Wicca Spell Book

Discover Spells for Healing, Wellbeing, Abundance, Wealth, Prosperity, Love and Relationships. A New and Improved Version of The First Book Wicca for Beginners.

© **Copyright Judith Guise 2019 - All rights reserved.**

The content contained within this book may not be reproduced, duplicated or transmitted without direct written permission from the author or the publisher.

Under no circumstances will any blame or legal responsibility be held against the publisher, or author, for any damages, reparation, or monetary loss due to the information contained within this book, either directly or indirectly.

Legal Notice:

This book is copyright protected. It is only for personal use. You cannot amend, distribute, sell, use, quote or paraphrase any part, or the content within this book, without the consent of the author or publisher.

Disclaimer Notice:

Please note the information contained within this document is for educational and entertainment purposes only. All effort has been executed to present accurate, up to date, reliable, complete information. No warranties of any kind are declared or implied. Readers acknowledge that the author is not engaging in the rendering of legal, financial, medical or professional advice. The content within this book has been derived from various sources. Please consult a licensed professional before attempting any techniques outlined in this book.

By reading this document, the reader agrees that under no circumstances is the author responsible for any losses, direct or indirect, that are incurred as a result of the use of information contained within this document, including, but not limited to, errors, omissions, or inaccuracies.

Table of Contents

Introduction..5

Chapter 1: The How to of Wicca Spells..........9

Chapter 2: Cautions and Warnings for New Beginners...15

    Chapter 3: Healing and Well-Being Spells.....22

Chapter 4: Relationship and Love Spells...33

Chapter 5: Abundance and Wealth Spells...43

Chapter 6: Candles and Spells....................52

Chapter 7: Crystals and Spells......................91

Chapter 8: Herbs and Spells......................117

Chapter 9: Essential Oils and Spells..........139

Conclusion..145

References..147

Introduction

You feel that you are unbalanced or a little blue. You feel that there is something missing from your life, but you're not sure what. One day, you are talking to a friend about the way you're feeling when they tell you about a Wiccan spell. They explain how this spell will help ease the negative feelings and bring more positivity into your life. With their guidance, you cast the spell. A couple of weeks later, you begin to notice the emotional changes within your life. You are thinking more clearly and focusing more on the positive side of life, even when something doesn't go your way.

This is the basis for Wiccan spells. They are here to help you reach your highest self and potential. They help ease the negativity in your life by focusing more on improving your self-care, confidence, and self-worth. Furthermore, they can strengthen bonds between you and your family members or friends. They can also help you find your soulmate or give you the courage to change your career.

Most of the chapters within this book are filled with Wiccan spells. However, it is important that you take the time to understand the important steps that come before each spell. Therefore, chapter 1 focuses on a brief introduction to Wiccan spells and gives you the how-to information when casting a spell. The basis of this chapter is guidelines for successfully performing a spell, such as calming your mind and visualization.

Chapter 2 is more of a cautionary tale. With any gift or skills, there are always warning labels attached. This chapter discusses the various warnings and dangers that come with casting spells. For example, it discusses how you can abuse your gift of casting if you are not careful. Wiccans use spells to help reach their best selves and provide others with a sense of relief when it comes to negativity in their lives. You always want to be careful how you perform a spell and make sure to thank the higher powers which helped you. Never use a spell in a negative light.

Chapter 3 focuses on health and well-being spells. These are spells which can help your mental and emotional state through healing. These spells are not meant to replace any medical attention or advice. These are simply spells which will help you create a better sense of balance, happiness, and focus on your overall well-being.

Chapter 4 focuses on love and relationship spells. These are some of the most common spells used in Wicca. They are also great spells for beginners, as they focus on any type of love, whether it is between friends, family members, or your significant other. You can also use spells in this category to boost your work office morale.

Chapter 5 focuses on wealth and abundance spells. Like love and relationship spells, the spells in chapter five look at several areas within your life. For instance, most people, when they think of wealth, imagine money. However, you can also be wealthy in love, happiness, and many other areas of your life. At the same time, the abundance spells can help you achieve more of what you desire as a human, such as compassion from other people. They can also focus on self-care. After all, as the spells in this book will teach you, self-compassion and self-love are just as important as receiving these factors from other people. You need an abundance of both in order to create a healthy balance.

Chapter 6 focuses on candles and spells. While not every spell uses candles, a majority of them do. This chapter will start by guiding you through the process of charging your candles. This is something you will always want to do before every spell. Unfortunately, I can't discuss specific spells associated with every color in this book, but I can discuss some of the most common colors used in spells.

Chapter 7 focuses on crystals and spells. Like the previous chapter, there are more crystals than I could discuss within the pages of this book. However, I do focus on a variety of crystals and try to give you a wide range of spells, from breaking free of addiction to helping you understand your dreams.

Chapter 8 discusses herbs and spells. There are many ways that you can use herbs within your spells. In fact, herbs are used in most spells, whether you use them to dress your candle, place them in a mixture, or create a tea from them. These spells can help you protect your new home, give you good luck while you are traveling, and help you heal your grief.

Chapter 9 focuses on using essential oils in spells. Of course, you can use oils in any spell, you just want to make sure that you are using oils which pertain to the outcome you want. When you use essential oils, you can focus on any type of spell, from love to luck. You can also look for ways to combine essential oils in order to create your own mix to use in certain spells.

Through this book, you will be able to learn a variety of spells to help you throughout your life. You will not only learn how you can help yourself, but how you can help other people. All of the spells within this book are suitable for beginners, however, anyone who is interested can use these spells.

Chapter 1: The How to of Wicca Spells

I won't spend a lot of time on this chapter, as I already discussed much of this in my previous book, *Wicca For Beginners: The Book of Spells and Rituals for Beginners to Learn Everything from A to Z. Witchcraft, Magic, Beliefs, History, and Spells*. In this book, I discussed the foundations of Wicca, how to set up your altar, honing your energy, Wiccan tools, and the basics of spells. This chapter is going to look beyond this. It is going to look at the "how-to" of Wicca spells. In other words, it is going to take you from the basics into how you will start to perform your chosen spell.

First, as the previous book discussed, you want to make sure you protect yourself, cleanse yourself, and are grounded before moving forward. If you have not done this, take a step back and read my previous book, as it discussed how to go about this in the last chapter. If you have done this and understand how to do so before each spell, then you can move on to the "how-to" of Wicca spells.

When you are going to perform your spell, safety is number one. You always want to perform the spell very carefully. You want to make sure that you have the time to energize your tools, perform the spell, and then close out the spell. You don't ever want to feel rushed, as you could find yourself missing a step or making a mistake.

When you find that you are ready to perform a spell, you want to make sure you start by asking for guidance. One of the reasons you do this is because you will see an image of a symbol or get a sense of which elements you should work with, such as air or water. However, you might also be given the advice not to perform the spell. If this is the feeling you get, then you need to take this advice. It might not be the right time or the divine might feel that you are not ready for the specific spell yet. There is also a possibility that you need to look at a different spell. Put your trust into the higher powers, as they will help guide you in the right direction.

Remember, when you perform a spell, you are tapping into your subconscious and unconscious mind. This is one of the biggest reasons why you always want to understand what you are doing, understand the consequences, and make sure that you are being safe. When you get into your unconscious mind, you are digging into pieces of you that you didn't know existed. There is nothing evil lurking there, but there are parts of your personality that you are unaware of. At the same time, you are going to run into emotions that you are unaware of about certain events or something else. In fact, this is something that you can look at when you find a spell isn't working as it should. Your unconscious is full of complications that can interrupt and influence the spells you are trying to perform. Therefore, instead of becoming frustrated that a spell isn't working, take time to learn a bit about yourself to find out why it isn't working.

While you want to follow the spells, you don't need to use them as a script. If you do this, you might not allow an open space for the divine to express itself. Think of it this way: if you need a new car, you are not going to ask for a specific car, such as a convertible. You are going to ask for any vehicle which will get you from point a to point b. When you allow the divine to express itself, it can help you grow and learn. In the end, you will trust the universe to give you the outcome that works for you within that moment.

Guidelines and Tips for Successful Spellcasting

Visualization

It is important that you can clearly visualize the outcome that you desire. Therefore, before you begin to cast a spell, you want to learn how to give clear images of your outcome. This outcome is the image that you will think about throughout the spell. It is the one that you will visualize from the beginning. In fact, you might start to visualize this image while your candles, crystals, and other tools are charging their energy for the spell.

To help you learn how to visualize objects, here is a simple exercise to use as a guide:

1. Find an object that you want to visualize. You can pick any object, from a vase to a rock. You don't have to pick something which has any type of emotional attachment to you.

2. Make your body relaxed and start to slowly breathe.

3. Take a few minutes to focus on the item. You don't need to pick it up or feel it. Simply allow your eyes and mind to focus on the image as you see it from where you are.

4. Close your eyes and see the image through your mind's eye. Think of the designs of the object, its shape, colors, and anything else. Make the image in your mind's eye as detailed as you can.

5. After a couple of minutes, open your eyes and take a look at the object. Compare the physical object to the image you created in your mind's eye. Do you notice any differences?

6. Take a couple of minutes and look at the object again, then close your eyes and repeat the exercise a few more times.

7. When you feel that your images match the object, put the object somewhere you can't see it and continue to visualize the object in your mind's eye.

Clear Your Mind

It is always important to clear your mind or give yourself a sense of calmness before you perform a spell. Not only will clearing your mind help with your focus, but it will also help you release any negative energy more easily.

One of the best ways to clear your mind is through meditation. Unless you want to, you don't have to sit or lay down in order to meditate. You can do this by standing in front of your altar or finding any place where you are comfortable.

When you meditate, you want to focus on your breathing, calming music, or the quietness of your space. You want to visualize that all the stress which is clouding your mind is leaving your body.

Another way to clear your mind is by taking several slow and deep breaths. You can mix this in with your meditation. The focus is to visualize all the negativity and stress leaving your body as you exhale and the calmness coming into your body as you inhale. Some people like to visualize keywords from situations which are stressful to them leaving their mind and body as they exhale.

You want to focus on clearing your mind until you feel relaxed and calm. You want to have an overall feeling of happiness take over.

Remember the Importance of Positivity

As you start reading through and casting spells, you will find that they all focus on making sure you are pushing the negative energy out of your body and bringing in the positive energy. It is important to remember to focus on this step in order for the spells to work. If you cast a spell and you still hold a lot of negative energy, the spell could backfire.

At the same time, you also need to realize that you might not be able to release all of the negative energy at once. While you will start to feel lighter almost immediately after performing the spell, there could be more negativity within your subconscious mind than you could ever realize. Therefore, you might find yourself taking a few weeks to fully feel the effects of the spell. You might also find yourself needing to repeat the spell a few weeks later. You do what you need to do in order to release the negativity within you. After all, the more negativity you release, the more space you will have for positivity.

Chapter 2: Cautions and Warnings for New Beginners

Before you go too far into Wiccan spells, you need to understand there are warnings when it comes to spells. Wiccans spells can become dangerous, but only if you allow them to. When it comes to performing spells, you are able to set the mood. For example, if you want to do something to get back at someone, you will be able to find a spell for that somewhere. However, this isn't what Wiccan spells are about. They are about helping you and other people. They will help you with your relationships, health, finding prosperity, and calmness.

You need to understand that this chapter isn't here to try to scare you off. It is here to make you aware of what else is out there and what can go wrong. There is a reason why you need to understand the spells, make sure to thank everyone and everything which helps you, and close out your spells. There is a reason why you need to do your research before you start to perform any spells. There is a reason why you need to recharge energy for yourself, your candles, your crystals, and other tools for your spells. This chapter is here to help you realize what certain guidelines exist so you don't find yourself trapped in any way.

Evil Does Exist In This World

When it comes to this world, there are many forms of good and there are many forms of bad. There are bad people just like there are good people. There are also bad entities, just like there are good entities. In general, people refer to these evil entities as demons or evil spirits. These evil entities bring negativity into the world. They are very strong and tend to feed off of our negative emotions. When you take a look at the dozens of spells within this book, you will notice that they work to bring forms of peace and positivity into your life. These are the emotions that evil tries to take away. They do this by focusing on your weak points and pushing your defenses down.

This is one reason you need to make sure you take precautions before you start your spell and then use your closing ritual. This will help protect yourself and those around you from the evil entities.

You Can Abuse Your Gift

You spend months learning about Wicca and how to perform spells. You do weeks of research and then you start to practice. You might even find help from a mentor or join a couple of social media sites which allow you to talk to other Wiccans. You notice improvements within your life from the first spell you perform. You start to believe in your gift. Soon, you start to believe that you are one of the best.

While you are an amazing person, it is important to not let your ego get too large. This can lead you to abuse your gift, as it makes you believe you are more powerful than the people around you. This can lead you to make poor choices, mistakes, or not think a spell through.

One way to help so you don't fall into the power trap is to always thank the universe or the higher powers you believe in for your gift. They are the ones who allowed you to have this gift. They are the ones who allowed you to build your gift. Without them, you wouldn't have this amazing gift. You wouldn't have been able to learn the art of spellcasting.

Another way to help is to make sure you always thank the powers that help you with your spell. For example, if you need the sunlight, thank the sun at the end of your spell. Without these natural powers, you wouldn't be able to complete the spell successfully. Never forget anyone or anything that helps you through your spells.

Always Know Your Consequences

Spellcasting is an art form. Magic is also as unpredictable as the weather. Take a moment to think about the last time you were in a severe thunderstorm warning. The radar showed that there was a storm heading your direction which would produce strong winds, heavy rain, hail, and possibly a tornado. The meteorologist states it will be near your area in 10 minutes. You start to prepare by gathering the items you need and head to a safe zone in your home, such as a room without windows or a basement. As you hear the rain start, you hear the meteorologist state that the storm is starting to weaken. It is no longer as strong as it was and is remaining south of your home about two miles.

This is an example of how unpredictable magic can be. Therefore, you need to make sure you do your research and understand the spell you are going to perform. You need to make sure that you know the consequences, such as what will happen if the spell works and what will happen if something goes wrong. You always need to remember that you are just learning the art form, which means you can make mistakes. In fact, even people who have used magic for decades can still make mistakes. You always want to be careful and understand what spell you are performing. If you need help, find a social media group, a mentor, or someone else who can guide you. There is never anything wrong with asking for help when you are in need.

Don't Listen to the Myths

There are a lot of myths that surround Wicca and spellcasting. These are myths that people have created over centuries out of fear, misunderstanding, and misguided ideas. Unfortunately, a lot of people will take the myths as truth because they don't want to take the time to understand, it's what they have believed their whole life, or many other reasons. This is one reason why it is important to do your research. You need to make sure you understand everything, including the myths.

For example, one of the oldest and most common myths is that everything with spells is evil. There are a lot of ways people have said this over the years. Some say that spellcasting is evil, witches are evil, and some even say that Wiccans are evil. Of course, none of it is true. Fortunately, this belief is starting to die down as people are beginning to understand the practice more and more. For example, more people today realize that Wiccans try to help people with their magic and spells. They don't want to harm anyone, as this is not their mission.

Never Leave a Candle Unattended

A lot of spells call for you to allow the candle to burn out. This means that you won't extinguish the candle when you are done with the spell. When you do this, you always want to make sure that you don't leave the candle unattended. You want to make sure that you are close by or able to keep your eye on the candle. Furthermore, you want to take all the precautions you can to eliminate any risk of fire. For example, don't allow anything near the flame, especially children or pets. Make sure that the flame has a lot of room and is not able to touch any type of object. This includes being too close to melt an object.

Herbs and Spells

Chapter 8 is dedicated to using herbs in your spells. It is important to remember that you always need to be safe when you are using herbs. While there are some herbs which are healthy for you to ingest, there are others which are toxic. Therefore, when using herbs for spells, you never want to ingest them into your body, unless you know the herb and what it can do to your body. Furthermore, if you are pregnant, you will want to discuss using any herbs with your doctor.

Essential Oils and Spells

There are a number of spells which use essential oils. In fact, chapter 9 is dedicated to using essential oils in your spells. Whenever you use oils, you need to use a small amount and be very careful. Oils are flammable, which can pose a risk of getting burned if you are not careful when mixing essential oils and candles in your spells.

Safety Is Always Number One

Above all, you always want to make sure that safety is number one. It doesn't matter what spell you are doing, if you feel that someone could be unsafe because you have children in the house or pets running around at the time, wait to perform your spell. Allow your candle, herbs, and crystals to energize and then perform the spell when you know the conditions are safe. Always remember safety for yourself, everyone around you, and your environment.

Chapter 3: Healing and Well-Being Spells

There are several types of healing in this world. Not only do you need to let your body heal when you receive a cut, broken bone, or fracture, but you also need to take time to heal your mind and emotions. Too often, people push away their emotions, as they feel they will get over it eventually. This is one of the biggest reasons why people find the need to use healing spells. After all, you can only push down your emotions so much before they become too much to bear.

When you learn Wiccan spells, you will find that most of them ask you to clear your mind or meditate before you begin the spell. This is because your well-being is one of the most important pieces of a successful spell. You need to be able to think clearly and positively in order to acquire the positive results you want. However, sometimes, you will need a little help in order to do this, which is when healing spells become an important part of your time.

Before I go further into this chapter, I want to take a moment to state that you should never use any type of spell over medical care and advice. If you need to visit your doctor because you are injured physically, depressed, anxious, or suffering mentally or emotionally in any way, then you need to see your primary care physician or therapist. Sometimes this is the step we need to take in order to bring ourselves back into balance.

A Spell to Release Any Negative Energy

You can find negative energy anywhere. This energy can attach itself to you without you realizing it. In fact, if you are an empath or a highly sensitive individual, you are more likely to feel someone else's emotions. It is important to understand that when you are feeling negative, it is going to affect your physical well-being. You may start to feel physically sick if you don't find a way to release the negative energy within you. While there are many ways to do this, one way is to use a spell to help release any built-up negative energy.

When it comes to the ingredients of this spell, you only need space and a red candle. Of course, you can also dress your candle with herbs or essential oils if you feel the need.

1. You will want to start by clearing your mind through a form of meditation. However, instead of closing your eyes, you want to light the candle and focus on the flame from the candle. You will do this because the flame from the candle will not only bring

you into focus, but will give you the power to overcome the negative energy within you.

2. Once you have become focused on the flame, you can then say the following or similar words:

"Any energy that is no longer helpful for me, I am now sending you home. Thank you for your presence, but please leave now."

You want to make sure that you say these words with conviction. You want to make the negative energies you no longer need believe that it is time to leave your soul.

3. You will need to repeat the words a few times. While you do this, you can also imagine the negativity leaving your body and even exiting your home through a window or the door.

4. As you continue to say the words, you will find yourself feeling lighter. You will also find that you are feeling more positive. Once you feel the negativity has left, you can extinguish the flame.

A Healing Spell

This is a general healing spell that you can use to help other people heal. Before you perform the spell, you will want to explain what you will have the person do.

You will also want to explain the spell to them, provided they have never used this spell before.

1. Before you start, you need to ensure that you have a clear mind.

2. Start by getting the person relaxed. You also want them to focus on clearing their mind, which they can do through meditation or just by breathing deeply for a couple of minutes. Make sure to help your patient, if they need help relaxing.

3. You will start to notice that the more you and your patient feel relaxed, the more positive you will feel. This is when you will start to notice that the spirits and higher powers are helping you and your patient heal.

4. Ask your patient to start talking about all the positive situations in their life. They can discuss their relationship, career, or anything else. Whatever happy and positive events that come to their mind are what they will discuss. The point is that these events need to be happening in your patient's life at the moment. They should not be past events or anything they are looking forward to.

5. Encourage your patient to close their eyes as you do the same thing. At this moment, you want to continue to focus on the healing powers that the spirits are bringing into the room. Thank the spirits for their presence and ask them to further help you and your patient heal.

6. As your patient continues to focus on the positives within their life, quietly discuss the factors that the patient has which need healing. Do not let the patient hear you state these factors to the healing spirits within the room. However, you want to make sure that these spirits are aware of your patient's issues which are affecting them.

7. If you know of any protective spells, you may recite a spell while visualizing a light of protection surrounding your patient.

Bringing Peace and Harmony to an Infected Space

One factor that many people don't think of when they are trying to heal is their environment. When we bring harmony into our atmosphere, we will be more likely to fully heal. Furthermore, our physical healing can speed up when our environment is at peace. This spell can be used for indoor and outdoor spaces. However, you will need to realize that when you are using this spell outdoors, it will be limited to your power and the power within the spell. Therefore, you want to perform the spell within the outdoor area you want to focus on.

The ingredients you will need for this spell are rosemary, thyme, and cinnamon. You will also want soil. For the most power, you will want to get plants of these herbs. However, if the plants are not available, then you can use dried herbs.

1. You want to make sure that you can reach the soil with both hands. If you have plants, place the pots in a line in front of you.

2. Cast your palms over each of the dried herbs or plants and say the following or similar words:

"Harmony and balance, ease and peacefulness. By the power of three, turbulence will cease."

3. As you are saying these words, visualize the peaceful energy coming from them, into your palms, and then into the plants or the dried herbs. You want to imagine an easy flow of energy.

4. Place the plants or the dried herbs into the space you wish to heal.

The spell will continue to work in the area as long as the plants are healthy. Of course, you will want to make sure that you take the time to reinforce the energies, as this will further help the space keep any peace.

Health and Well-Being Spell

This spell is a general spell to help improve your well-being. Again, it is important you remember that none of these spells are meant to replace a physician.

The ingredients for this spell are rosemary, sandalwood, juniper, honey, one green candle, one yellow candle, an empty jar, yellow ribbon, and sea salt.

1. Take a healing bath or get a bowl to fill with healing water where you can wash your hands and face.

2. Add the sea salt, rosemary, juniper, and sandalwood into your water.

3. While the water is running, state the following or similar words:

"Grant healing powers to this water. Bring wellness, health, and vitality. I will cleanse and bring positivity toward me."

4. As you are soaking in the water, visualize the healing powers entering your body. Once you are finished, head to your altar or sacred space.

5. Cast your circle and call forth the healing powers, particularly from Earth.

6. Light the green and yellow candle. As you do this, say the following or similar words:

"Light of healing, bless this work."

7. In the empty jar, add the rosemary, three tablespoons of honey, sea salt, sandalwood, and juniper essential oils. Make sure you have enough honey, as this is the symbol of the healing powers.

8. Pour in a few drops of wax from the yellow and green candles. As you do this, say the following or similar words:

"Healing earth, light, and bee let the healing energy flow through me."

9. In a clockwise direction, slowly stir the mixture. Focus on the healing energies as they start flowing through your body. They might start at your hands as they come from the jar, work their way up into your shoulders, your chest, and then spread into other areas of your body. Take time to visualize the healing energy flowing through you.

10. Place the lid onto the jar and tie a yellow ribbon around it. You should make a bow with the ribbon.

11. Make sure to thank the healing energy and Earth for their assistance in this spell. You can either extinguish the candles or allow them to burn out themselves.

Keep the jar in your home or with you for a few days. Once you feel the healing energy is starting to work, you can discard the mixture by pouring it on the earth. You should do this close to your home so you can continue to feel the energy work.

A Spell to Help Us Cleanse and Purify

Sometimes we find ourselves feeling under the weather because we haven't taken the time to cleanse and purify our bodies. This is necessary, as we often carry negative emotions within us. Most of the time, we don't notice these emotions until they start to become a problem. By taking the time to cleanse and purify yourself now and then, you are eliminating the negativity from your soul, which can help you remain healthy and happy. It is important to note that you can use this spell on yourself or your living space.

The ingredients for this spell are a silver pen or marker, one white candle, one blue candle, a rock that you have collected from the seashore, sandalwood incense, and a crystal of your choosing.

For the best results, you should perform this spell during a full moon. If you are unable to get to the sea to pick up a rock or pebble, you can find another one within nature. You might be able to find one in the country next to a lake or in another peaceful setting.

1. If you are able to visit the sea before performing this spell, you will want to make sure that you notice

the waves and sounds of the ocean. Take time to smell the air and honor the amazing source of nature.

2. Cast a circle in your chosen space.

3. Light the sandalwood and allow the smell to fill your area.

4. Take your rock or pebble from the sea and place it between the palms of your hands. Take time to clear your mind as you feel the ocean or the sounds of nature where you picked up the rock.

5. Visualize that the energy from this rock is removing any negative energy from your body. The rock is starting to cleanse and purify you. As you visualize the waves of the ocean or hear the sounds of nature, say these or similar words:

"Goddess of the sea, thank you for your beauty and bounty. Allow your waves to wash over me as they cleanse my body and soul. Bring your protection to cover me. Allow your healing powers to go through me. For the best good. So let it be."

6. Take time to feel nature and yourself becoming one.

7. When you feel that this connection is strong, take your silver marker and draw a pentacle on the rock.

8. Thank nature, the sea, and the powers which helped you with this spell.

9. Place your rock in a safe place. You will use this rock to meditate every time you feel that you need to cleanse and purify yourself.

Chapter 4: Relationship and Love Spells

Love and relationship spells are probably some of the most popular spells people think of. In fact, these are some of the first spells beginners cast. One important factor to remember is that some relationship and love spells focus on the events that can take place to make the love between you and your significant other grow stronger, while other spells will focus on personality characteristics. When a spell tells you to focus on one or the other, you want to follow what the spell states. For example, if you are to focus on how you will create a stronger bond between you and your significant other, you don't want to focus on how they can change their personality in order to suit you. This can make the spell backfire.

A Spell for Healing a Fractured Relationship

When you are looking to dive into Wiccan relationship spells, the best ones for you to start with focus on your current relationship. This spell is great for people who feel their current relationship is complicated.

The ingredients for this spell include a fire-resistant bowl, one pink candle, one white candle, a lighter or matches, a long string cut into two pieces, paper, and a writing utensil.

1. Take your paper and write two letters which correspond to the higher powers you are calling to help with this spell.

2. In the first letter, you will want to write about what problems you are having in your current relationship. Anything which has caused you and your significant other to argue or disagree is important. You can also discuss any events which have hurt you emotionally or mentally. You want to make sure to discuss everything, no matter how hurtful it is to you. The more emotion you pour into the letter, the stronger the spell will become.

3. In the second letter, you will write about how you want to address and repair these problems. You will discuss your ideas on how to establish a better bond between you and your significant other. Dig into your imagination as you discuss ways in which you will resolve arguments. Once you have finished writing this letter, take a moment to reflect. Notice any changes in your energies as the higher powers have already started to help you.

4. In this spell, the white candle is used as a symbol of peace and the pink candle as a symbol of love. You will light both candles as you hold the letters in your hand.

5. Take your first letter and place it in the fireproof bowl.

6. Use the matches or lighter to set the letter on fire. Watch as the smoke rises from the letter. This is a way to let go of the tension of negativity which has filled your relationship. While you are watching the smoke rise, say these or similar words:

"Sacred flames, take these negative energies away. Allow my relationship to begin anew today."

7. Re-read the second letter in order to create a clear visualization of the process you are going to put into action.

8. Take the two pieces of string and tie them together tightly. Pull both sides of the string to make sure that the knot will not come undone. This is a symbol of your relationship.

9. Fold the second letter in half twice.

10. Wrap the string around the letter. As you do this, say these or similar words:

"Goddess and God above, allow me and my love to reunite. Bring loving peace and harmony into our lives as our bond increases."

11. Take both the burned letter and second letter outside and find a tree. You will want to find a tree which pulls you in through your energies. Once you find this tree, dig a small hole and bury the letters in front of the tree. You will start to notice your

relationship becoming more positive as the letters start to mix in with the earth.

Blind Date Ritual Bath

Sometimes, one of the most anxious times is when you are about to go on a blind date. These moments make many people feel worried, because you don't know anything about the person. While you are usually set up through a mutual friend, this doesn't always ease any worries. Therefore, you might want to take part in a spell before going on a blind date. With this spell, you will make sure that you have a good time, as your self-confidence and beliefs in making sure you have a great night will increase.

The ingredients for this spell are one tablespoon of chamomile, one tablespoon of hibiscus, one tablespoon of red clover, one piece of citrine, candles for atmosphere, three tablespoons of sea salt, and five drops of lavender essential oil. You can also use fewer ingredients by using teaspoons instead of tablespoons.

1. When the bathtub is a quarter of the way full with water, dump in the sea salt.

2. When the bathtub is halfway full, drop in the essential oil and the crystal.

3. When you are about ready to shut off the water, add the herbs.

4. Light your candles and turn off any other lighting before getting into the bathtub.

5. As you sit in the tub, you will want to relax and then let go of your anxieties about meeting your blind date.

6. Relax in the bath for about 20 to 25 minutes. Continue to sit there as you drain the water, because this will increase the strength of the essential oil and herbs.

7. Take your crystal out of the tub and carry it with you on your blind date.

New Friendships Spell

There is more to love spells than romantic interests. This is because there are different forms of love. There is the love between you and your significant other, and there is the love between you and your friends. Therefore, you can also use love spells in order to strengthen your friendships or create new friendships, which is what this spell aims to do. It doesn't matter if you recently moved to a new area or just need new friends, this spell can help you accomplish it.

Most people say the best time to cast this spell is during the waxing moon. However, like all the other spells, you can perform it any time. The ingredients you will need for this spell are one small rose quartz, lavender essential oil, and one yellow spell candle.

1. Rub essential oil around the sides of the candle.

2. Lay the stone in your dominant hand. This means if you write with your right hand, lay the stone in this hand. Lay your other hand on top of the stone.

3. Close your hands together and close your eyes. Take a few minutes to visualize positive people around you having fun.

4. Once you have the comforting and fun feeling, take a deep breath and open your eyes.

5. Lay the stone in front of the candle.

6. Light the candle as you say these or similar words:

"Friendships true and new, let our kindred souls meet."

7. Place the stone in a certain spot in your home where you will see it often. Remember to grab the stone every time you leave your home.

Release Negative Attachments Spell

Sometimes we meet and start a relationship with the wrong person. While the relationship will end, you still carry negative emotions and attachments from the relationship. This is often referred to as "baggage" and is something which can cause problems within your future relationships. Furthermore, continuing to carry these negative emotions is not going to help your mental state or overall well-being. Therefore, it is always best to do what you can to release any negativity from a relationship. This includes any friendships which end badly.

It is important to note that this spell is not meant to take all your negativity away immediately. This is often something that takes time. The true aim of this spell is to keep you from focusing on the negative, which will help you get over everything and release this type of energy. It doesn't matter if the other person continues to try to reach you or cause problems. This spell will become more powerful than anything they can do to try to bring you down.

Before you start this spell, it is important to note that you need to focus your energy on yourself and not the other person. You need to build your own positive energy back up in order to get over any negative situation.

The ingredients you will need for this spell are a 1 inch by 7 inch piece of paper, one black candle, a writing utensil, more paper, sandalwood or sage incense, and a fireproof dish.

1. Light the incense.

2. Take the large sheets of paper and start freewriting. Make sure you don't dwell on the negativity that is surrounding the situation, but the whole deal. Your plan is to remove the thoughts from your mind, so you can focus on more positive thoughts.

3. Take the smaller piece of paper and write the name of the person you are focusing on. You will also write one sentence which discusses the summary of the conflict.

4. Roll the paper as you would a loose scroll.

5. As you light the candle, take a deep breath or two and say the following or similar words:

"On this night, with this candle, I let go of my need to be right. Within this open space, fill with healing peace."

6. Light the scroll on fire and place it in the fireproof bowl. Let the smoke rise from the bowl.

7. Leave the candle to burn out on its own for the best results. However, you can extinguish the candle if you are unable to watch it.

8. Once the ashes are cooled, you can throw them outside to become one with the earth. Use these ashes to visualize how you are releasing the negative attachments every time you find yourself re-thinking about these attachments.

Conjure a Romantic Interest Spell

There is someone out there for you, and this spell will help you find this person. This isn't a spell that will bring love into the relationship, however, it will bring an interested partner where the love between you two can blossom.

Many people believe that the best time to cast this spell is the week after a full moon. The ingredients for this spell are one red candle, three white candles, petals from a red rose, and a glass of brewed mint tea.

1. Take the three white candles and form a triangle in front of you. Make sure the base of the triangle is closest to you.

2. Place the red candle in the middle of the triangle.

3. Do not light the candles, as you want to sprinkle the rose petals around the candles. As you are sprinkling the petals around the triangle, state the following or similar words:

"Goddess of love, I invoke thee. Goddess of love, I invoke thee. Please help find my soulmate. Goddess of love, I invoke thee so I can cure my loneliness. Such is my will."

4. Light the candles, starting with the white candle on your left, then the point of the triangle, and then the right base. You will then light the red candle.

5. Drink your tea. As you feel the tea flow down your throat, think of the warmth the tea brings. Visualize this warmth turning into energy within you. Once you have finished the tea, place the cup to the side.

6. Extinguish the candles, starting with the bottom right at the base of the candle and go the opposite way you did lighting them. Extinguish the red candle last.

7. Pick up the rose petals and place them into a container. These petals are now energized and they will be helpful to carry around with you or be placed safely in your home. Keep the petals for at least a week.

8. Once the week is over, find flowing water, such as a river or a stream, and place the petals within the water and watch the petals float away.

Chapter 5: Abundance and Wealth Spells

We all have dreams and goals. We all want a life where we don't have to live paycheck to paycheck. We want to feel financially secure and be able to put money toward saving, investing, or retirement. Sometimes we will find ourselves wishing for a better vehicle, home, or nicer possessions. While these wants are part of being human, you don't want to focus on this when you are performing these spells. You never want to abuse the powers that have been given to you from the universe or a higher power.

These spells are meant to enhance your life and well-being. It is also important to remember that there are many types of abundance and wealth. While we often think of money, there is also abundance and wealth with love, family, friends, and positive emotions. There is wealth in a positive mindset. There are spells which will focus on giving you more financial wealth, and there are also spells which will make you realize that you are worth what you have been given in your life. This mindset is more important than any amount of money. Therefore, if you feel that you are struggling with your mindset, this spell will help you through this troubling time.

Dandelion Prosperity Spell

While most people get tired of dandelions, there is great symbolism within this part of nature. Instead of mowing over the dandelions in your yard, take a moment to focus on how beautiful they look. The yellow symbolizes the sun and fire as the name "lion" is a symbol of strength. Once your dandelion has turned to its cotton ball phase, the seeds symbolize our intentions being carried with the wind. The stem of the dandelion can be used in order to make a healing tea.

The ingredients you will need for this spell are a flowering dandelion, a citrine crystal, a writing utensil, paper, and glass. This spell is best performed when the sun is shining brightly outside. However, if you need to perform the spell and it is a cloudy or wintery day, you will want to light a yellow and white candle in order to represent the Sun and its warmth.

1. Cast your circle or visualize a glowing white light around you.

2. Take the dandelion and place it into your glass, which you will then fill with clean water.

3. If it fits, place your crystal in your glass. If it doesn't fit, place it beside the glass or somewhere next to you.

4. Focus on your paper and write the following or similar words:

"I wish to add more prosperity into my life."

You can then focus on the areas which you want to prosperity to go. For example, you might wish to bring more compassion into your relationship or you might wish to bring more happiness into your career.

5. Focus your attention on your dandelion. Visualize how the Earth's powers helped the dandelion grow and how the Sun's warmth gave the dandelion its nutrients.

6. Take your piece of paper and place it into the glass.

7. At this point, you can choose to end the spell and discard the ingredients. However, you can also decide to leave the dandelion on your altar and continue with the spell once the dandelion turns into its cotton ball state.

8. Bring the glass and ingredients outside and find a spot to bury the piece of paper. As you do this, say the following or similar words:

"I commit my intent to this earth. Allow for the prosperity to grow within my life."

9. Dump out the water.

10. Hold the dandelion in one hand and your crystal in the other. Then blow on the dandelion to release the seeds. After you do this, say the following or similar words:

"With these seeds, I project my will. Allow new opportunities to find me near and far."

11. Thank all of the energies, especially the dandelion, which helped you with this spell. Place your crystal near your bedside or carry it with you, as this will allow you to feel the prosperity grow.

Spell for New Opportunities

This is a spell which you will want to use when you want to advance in your career, find a new career, or find more opportunities within your life. You should not use this spell in order to find a new love interest. If this is your focus, you will want to look at a relationship and love spell.

Many people feel that this spell is best when you perform it under a new or full moon.

The ingredients you will need to perform this spell are sandalwood or bergamot essential oil, citrine, candles, and an image which represents the new opportunity you want, such as your dream job.

1. Light any candles which represent earth and air. The colors of these candles are generally white, green, and yellow.

2. Place a crystal over the image and visualize reaching your desired career or goal.

3. As you are visualizing, say these or similar words:

"Wind and soil, air and earth, please send me a loving toil. I draw the work which pleases best, in love and strength."

4. As you say these words, take the essential oil and anoint yourself at pressure points, such as your wrists, third eye area, and temples.

5. Blow out the candles or allow them to burn out on their own. You may keep the image with you or place it in your home. Make sure to thank the powers which helped you with this spell.

A Simple Money Spell

There are many spells which focus on bringing more money in your direction. Some of them focus on good luck, while others focus on gambling. This spell simply focuses on bringing more money your way through other means.

First, it is important for me to say that while simple is in the title, this spell is often a bit challenging for beginners. However, this is not because the spell itself is difficult. It is because you are not sure how the money is going to come your way. You might get a promotion at work or you might be hired on for freelance work. Someone could also give you money. When it comes to how you receive the money, the options are endless. Because of this, the spell takes a lot of patience.

The ingredients for this spell are a gold ring, a gold necklace chain, and three yellow or gold colored candles. Many people feel that the best time to perform this spell is during a new moon.

1. Take the three candles and create a triangle from them right in front of you. Make sure the base of the triangle is closest to you.

2. Light the candles in a clockwise direction, starting with the bottom left candle.

3. Place your gold ring and necklace chain in the middle of the triangle.

4. Now, you want to visualize wealth. You will start with the gold ring and necklace. You will then move on to more expensive items. Don't focus on how you could get these new valuable items. You simply want to focus on acquiring the items.

5. You will want to spend about five to seven minutes visualizing. As you do this, you will say the following or similar words:

"Abundance, prosperity, and wealth, come into my life and give me freedom. So it will be. Let it be."

You will want to say this about ten to twelve times.

6. Take the gold ring and place it on a finger. Then take the gold necklace and wear it.

7. Extinguish the candles in the opposite way you lit them. This means you will start with the bottom right candle and go counter-clockwise.

8. Continue to wear the ring and necklace as often as you can. The more you wear them, the more you will feel the energies which will bring you more of the wealth you desire.

Bring Success into Your Work Environment Spell

Sometimes one of the best ways to bring more wealth into your life is to look toward your career. You can use spells such as this one to help create a better work environment, give you more self-esteem, or allow you to gain more determination to succeed. This can often lead you to receive promotions or a raise, which will help increase your financial wealth. Furthermore, if you are able to increase the overall morale of your workplace, you are able to gain a different type of wealth which will include creating more positivity for other people as well.

You don't need to use this spell only to bring more abundance into your current position. You can also use this spell if you are looking for a new career or would like to start your own business.

The ingredients for this spell include one white candle, four green candles, an image of your goal or a picture of the person you wish to send abundance to, your favorite essential oil, two green fluorite stones, bay leaves, amber incense, a bowl, and a collection of various coins. You want to make sure the coins hold different values.

1. Anoint your hands with the essential oil. Then you will want to wash and dry your hands.

2. Place the four green candles in front of you at the cardinal points.

3. Place the white candle directly in front of you.

4. Place the incense bowl where you can easily access it.

5. Place the stones, bay leaves, and coins into the bowl.

6. Place the photo directly in front of the white candle.

7. Bring yourself into a meditative state.

8. Take the incense and move the stick around the candles in a clockwise manner.

9. Light the white candle, the green candles, and then light the incense with the flame from the white candle.

10. Continue to focus on the spell and visualize success as you allow the wax to melt on the white candle. Once enough wax has melted, pour a few drops onto the picture. Then, hold the bowl in your hand and state the following or similar words:

"Success is coming my way. Prosperity is coming my way. So let it be."

11. Set the bowl down and allow the candle to burn. Place the incense back in its spot and start to visualize how the success and prosperity will come your way. Instead of imagining the end result, visualize the route it will take. For example, you can imagine yourself working hard in order to get the promotion you dream about.

12. Continue to visualize until you have a clear process in your mind. You may then extinguish the candles, starting with the green candles and ending with the white candle.

If you wish, you can carry the picture with you in your purse or place it in your desk at work. If you feel that the spell is wearing off, you will want to repeat the process.

Chapter 6: Candles and Spells

Candles are important when it comes to Wiccan spells. You can receive energies from certain candles which will help strengthen your spells. There are two sources of energy which will come from your candles. The first is the vibrations from the colors. The second energy is the Element of Fire. Many people believe beginners should start with candle spells, as they are some of the easiest to work with.

There are various sizes of candles which will be used in these spells. For instance, some will use pillar candles while others will use spell candles and tea light candles. It is important to note that many people believe you should let the candle burn out on its own. However, there are many spells which call for you to extinguish the candle. If the spell calls for this, then this is what you need to do. However, you do not want to use the candle for another spell. Instead, just use it again for the atmosphere you were going for with the spell. When extinguishing a candle, you don't want to blow it out unless you have to. In which case, you then want to thank the Element of Fire before you do. If you have a candle snuffer, it is best to use this. Otherwise, simply wave the candle out with your hand.

Charge Your Candles

Before you begin any spell, you always need to take time to charge the items you will use. This means that you will want to charge any candles. In order to do this, you can hold the candle in your hands, usually between your palms, and focus your energy into the wax of the candle. However, there are other ways that you can charge your candles. Some of the ways to charge candles will take time, so you need to make sure that you have a specific way to charge your candles a few days before you plan on performing the spell.

Herbs

When you use herbs to charge your candles, you will need a combination of herbs or a single herb. First, you will want to charge your herb, which you can do by holding them in your hand and visualizing the herb growing. You will place your herbs in a mason jar, which is big enough to hold your candle. Then you will add your candle and tightly close the lid. Gently shake the jar and leave it on your altar or another safe place for a couple of days. You will want to remember to spend time with the contents in the jar every day. Don't take the candle or herbs out until you are ready to perform the spell. Instead, hold the jar and focus your energy on it. You can visualize the ingredients coming together, charging, or connecting. You can also just take your time to energize the ingredients yourself by focusing your energy into the jar. You will want to make sure to use both the herbs and candle in your spell. For example, you can use the herbs as dressing for your candle.

Light Meditation

Hold the candle in between your palms. When you are relaxed, close your eyes and imagine the color you want to bring into your candle. You can use a candle which is the same color you are visualizing or another candle, such as white. In your mind's eye, imagine how this color is growing from your heart chakra and then starts moving through your chest, shoulders, arms, hands, and then into your candle. When the color gets into the wax of your candle, imagine the candle lighting up with your chosen color. Continue to do this until your candle is fully charged. The only person who will be able to tell this is done is yourself, as you will be able to feel it.

Oils

Oil is an ingredient which you can use to charge your candles as well as include them in your spells. Of course, there are also spells which focusing specifically on essential oils. When you use essential oils to charge your candle, you want to pour a small amount of oil onto your candle. You will then let it sit for several hours before you rub the oil into the candle. Remember, oil is flammable, so you want to make sure everything is safe and not use a lot of oil when you go to light the candle.

Crystals

When you use crystals to charge your candles, you will want to give your ingredients a week to charge together. Crystals and candles often go hand in hand when it comes to spells. In fact, there are several spells where you will use both. When you are using crystals to charge your candles, you will want to take five crystals and create a five-pointed star or pentacle. You will place your candle in the middle of the shape. Once your week has come to an end and you're about to perform the spell, you will need to cleanse the crystals if you won't use them in the spell.

Red

Red is known to be the color which brings love, passion, energy, relationships, and lust. It is one of the strongest colors which can be used positively and negatively. For example, red can be used as a symbol of anger and it can be used as a symbol for love. At the same time, red can be the color of survival—think of how your blood or heart is red.

When you use red candles in a spell, you are focusing on more than improving your relationships. You are also focusing on increasing your motivation, willpower, physical energy, determination, physical healing, and ambition. You can use red in order to increase these energies in your personal or professional life. You can also use red to help boost your confidence and leadership skills.

Sunlight Ritual to Increase Your Physical Energy

We all feel exhausted from time to time. You might find that you are lacking more energy throughout your day than normal. While there might be medical reasons for this, which is why you always want to get a check-up from your primary care physician, you might also be able to help increase your physical energy through a spell. The Sunlight Ritual for Physical Energy spell can often help. However, as stated before, no spell should be used as a replacement for medical purposes.

When reaching into your mindset for this spell, you will want to focus on how there are many people with you. Think of all the people who have lived throughout history across the world, from the Aztecs to the Europeans crossing the sea to come to the new land.

When you are going to perform this spell, it is always best to do so under direct sunlight and outdoors. However, when this is not possible, you will want to visualize sunlight beaming down on you and your altar. Feel the warmth of the Sun of your face, shoulders, and your body.

For this spell, you will need three red candles, work atmosphere candles, and three large squares of tin foil. For your work atmosphere candles, you can use red, orange, yellow, pink, or white.

1. Using each piece of tin foil, make a sturdy holder around each red candle. You will want to form the shape of a triangle around you with the candles. You also want to make sure that you are in the center of the triangle.

2. When you are standing in the center of the triangle, light each candle. Make sure you focus on the light of the Sun reflecting off the tin foil and the light from the flames.

3. Hold your palms outward, close your eyes, and feel the warmth of the Sun.

4. Start meditating with the energy from the light. With your eyes still closed, imagine the energies of the light coming into your body, starting at your feet. Allow this energy to slowly work up your body. Visualize this energy going to your knees, your hips, your chest, shoulders, and all the way to the top of your head.

5. Open your eyes and continue to feel the solar energy inside of you.

6. Before you extinguish the candles, make sure to say a couple of words of thanks to the Sun and the never-ending energy it provides.

7. You can recycle the tin foil or save it for the next time you perform the sunlight ritual.

Power of Will Victory Charm

Sometimes we need a little willpower in order to start a new task or continue with our task. It doesn't matter if you are about to start a new job, exercise routine, or just need to give your house a deep clean, the Power of Will Victory Charm spell will help you accomplish this task.

For this spell, you will need a red magic charm. Many people like to use Red Jasper, however, you can choose any red stone. You also need one red pillar candle, a ritual carving tool such as a crystal point, and anointing oil, which is optional.

1. Take your carving tool and candle, and carve a symbol into your candle. This symbol needs to symbolize the goal you want to achieve. For example, you could carve a "V" for victory or "P" for power. You could also carve an image of your goal. Whatever symbol you decide to carve into your candle, it has to hold significant value for you toward this goal.

2. If you decide to use the oil, you will now want to anoint your candle.

3. Take your red stone and hold it between your palms.

4. Close your eyes and begin to visualize yourself accomplishing your task. Make sure you really imagine completing the task and feel victorious.

5. Once you have completed your visual, place the red stone in front of the candle.

6. Light the candle and repeat the following phrase three times:

"I am willpower. I am worthy. I am success. I am energy."

7. Allow the candle to burn out on its own, as it will continue to energize your stone as it burns. Once the candle is done burning, place the stone in your pocket and keep it with you whenever you need energy in order to fulfill your task.

Passionate Relationship Spell

You are ready to find a significant other. There are tons of love spells you can use. However, one of the key steps you want to take is to make sure you imagine your ideal partner. While most people will imagine the best personality characteristics of the person, it could help to imagine some flaws.

Everyone has them, therefore, if you imagine these in your ideal partner, you will be able to establish what you truly want.

The qualities of your lover will need to be in your mind before you start preparing the spell. This is because during the spell, you will write down the qualities and have a clear vision.

Remember, there are two people in a relationship. Therefore, you don't just want to focus on your ideal partner. You will also need to focus on yourself. Think about self-esteem and how important this is to a relationship and not just love. You need to focus on positive qualities as much as possible.

The tools you will need for the Passionate Relationship Spell are cinnamon, rose, or jasmine essential oil, a red spell candle, a ritual carving tool, a red writing utensil, paper, wax paper, and scissors.

1. Carve a symbol of love, such as a heart, into the red candle.

2. Anoint the red candle with your chosen oil.

3. Light the candle so the wax can start to melt.

4. Cut two shapes of a heart out of paper. Try to make them about the size of your palms. On one of the hearts, write the most important qualities of your significant other down with the red pen or marker. On the other heart, write down the list of qualities you will offer to your significant other.

5. Place the hearts within the palm of your hands and hold them there for a while. Imagine you and the other person coming together to create a new love.

6. Place the hearts, overlapping, onto a sheet of wax paper. As you talk out loud, you will list all of the qualities you wrote down.

7. With each quality you state, you will pour a drop of wax onto the hearts. This will seal them together.

8. Once you have completed listing off the qualities, you will then say these words or something similar:

"Passionate minds, passionate hearts, passionate souls. We are now together. So let it be."

9. Take the hearts and place them in a special place within your home or on your altar. Let the candle burn out on its own.

Green

Green is the color of the heart chakra, which means it acts like a mediator between the realms of thought and emotion. It also focuses on compassion, love, self-love, and relationships. While most people think of money when they see the color green, it is also a sign of good luck. Of course, people use the color green when they are trying to increase luck or their financial well-being. However, green is also associated with life. It shows that plants and nature are alive and well. Therefore, green can also be a sign of physical fertility. Green and the Element of Earth are often together.

Candlelight Fertility Spell

If you are a woman trying to conceive a child, you know that there are a lot of old wives tales, herbs, and medicines that are known to help. However, there is also a Candlelight Fertility Spell. Many women have performed this spell for themselves or a friend, who later found out they were pregnant. It reaches into the powers of the universe to help increase a woman's fertility through green candles, which focus on bringing abundance and good luck.

When you are preparing for the Candlelight Fertility Spell, you need to make sure that you are able to clear your mind. You need to let go of any negativity, including negative thoughts. It might help if you take the time to meditate and imagine all the negativity leaving your body. This is important because the magic from the spell will manifest in your body.

When you carve the symbol into the candle, you will want to make sure that it is personal for you. You don't need to pick a specific symbol, but it should represent your outcome. You could carve a picture of a baby or "B" for baby. Whatever you do, you want to make sure that it is the symbol that you want to represent fertility.

In order to perform this spell, you will need a carving tool, a large green candle, clary sage or geranium essential oil, and the symbols which represent fertility.

1. While you are carving your symbol of fertility into the candle, make sure you are imagining your body joining with the body of your significant other in order to create new life.

2. Anoint the candle with oil.

3. Once you and your significant other come together in your mind, you will want to light the candle.

4. If you are unable to conceive, repeat this spell. You can continue to repeat the spell until conception occurs.

Lucky Penny Employment Spell

Job hunting can be stressful and frustrating, especially if you don't have a lot of experience. For example, you just graduated from college or you are now looking at working away from home as your children are in school. Sometimes you don't have the right amount of experience, even if you have a certain degree. Other times you might be looked over because you don't know the right people.

The Lucky Penny Employment Spell will not help you get to know the right people in time for your job interview. However, it will help you acquire good luck for your future job interviews and help you land employment. This is because the spell focuses on the positive energy within you, which is a major factor when job hunting. The more stressful job hunting is and the more you receive rejection emails and letters, the more you start to feel negative about the whole situation. This will influence your performance in job interviews. Therefore, you can use this spell to help you maintain the positivity which is desired.

For this spell, you will need to use a spell candle and pour wax. Therefore, you might want to put down wax paper or something to protect your altar from any wax. Along with a green spell candle, you will need a new penny, wax paper, and journal paper (both of these items are optional), and lavender, clove, or patchouli essential oil.

1. Take the new penny and anoint both sides with oil.

2. Place the penny face up in front of your green candle.

3. Light the candle. Then imagine what it will be like to work at your dream job for several minutes as you stare into the melting wax of the candle.

4. If you have chosen to use journal paper, take time to free write what your dream job will be. What will your responsibilities be? Write down how well you will be able to perform these duties.

5. After you have finished writing and feel successful with your vision, you will want to drip three drops of green candle wax onto the coin. If you have chosen to use wax paper, make sure it is placed underneath the coin before you tip your candle. Remember to be careful so you don't burn yourself with any candle wax.

As you are dripping candle wax onto the coin, say "It is done. The job is now mine." You will then place the candle back into its holder and allow it to burn out on its own.

6. The next time you go to a job interview, you will carry the coin with you in your purse or pocket.

Magic Cash Spell

This is one of the many spells around that will help you increase the flow of cash. Most of the spells are similar, however, this one uses essential oils and a green spell candle. The best essential oil to use is Patchouli. You will also need a green rubber band and a five-dollar bill.

1. Anoint the candle with the essential oil.

2. Take the five-dollar bill and fold it lengthwise. You will then wrap it around the candle and secure the bill with the rubber band. Make sure to leave space between the five-dollar bill and the candle wick so the bill doesn't catch on fire.

3. Hold the bill between the palms of your hands. Take time to imagine you are living comfortably. While you are not rich, all of your basic needs are met. You can pay your bills on time, buy groceries, purchase gas to get back and forth to work, and you are able to have some money left over for yourself. You can even imagine a little bit going into savings every month.

4. Once this image is solid in your mind and your emotions are strong towards the image, you will want to repeat similar words three times:

"Above and below, money in my life does flow. The ground to the sky, from shore to shore, money brings me more."

5. Light the candle and allow it to burn until it reaches the five-dollar bill.

6. Extinguish the candle and allow the wax to cool before you remove the bill.

7. Place the bill in your wallet, preferably in a special place so you won't spend it. Remember the image and feeling you created every time you see the bill. Remind yourself that you are working toward this lifestyle.

Pink

Pink is the color of love, mixed with white and red. Pink can be used for any type of love, from friendships to romantic. It can even be used to bring a more gentle and cheerful environment to your job. It holds the energies for gentleness and cheerfulness. When people think of pink, they often think of flowers or something lovely. Therefore, this is the type of energy that pink candles tend to give. In general, when you need to use a spell which focuses on caring for other people, pink is usually the color you want.

You can also use pink to bring more harmony into your home. If you feel that your life and the energy within your home has been chaotic and stressful, or if you find that you and your significant other are arguing often or your children aren't getting along as well, you might want to bring more pink into your home, specifically focusing on a spell with pink candles. You can also use pink to help with self-improvement. It's a color which is associated with new beginnings. It gives you the energy to succeed. It also helps you remain calm so you can think more rationally, which always help with self-improvement and success.

Pink candles are often used in spells that focus on children and their health. This is because, even though society says pink is for girls, it has been associated with babies for centuries. It's often been used to help protect children.

The Element of Fire is associated with the color pink. The spells within this book which focus on pink are used to help children, strengthen friendships, romances, and self-love.

Strawberry Salad Romance Spell

The Strawberry Salad Romance Spell can be used for two different romances. First, it can be used to spice up your romantic life. Second, it can be used to establish a new romance. The trick is you need to focus on the experiences you want to have and not how you want the person to act. If you focus on personality characteristics, your spell is not going to work.

When it comes to the Strawberry Salad Romance Spell, you need to do what feels right. This means that you can change the ingredients in the spell to your liking. You can also add pieces into the spell, such as romantic music, incense, or anything else that you feel will give it a specialized romantic twist.

For this spell, you will need at least two pink candles, two cups of strawberries which you will cut in half, a half cup of blueberries, one cup of raspberries, one work candle which is pink or red, one cup of watermelon which you will cut into bite-sized pieces, a half cup of pitted cherries, one and a half teaspoons each of honey and chopped mint leaves, and three teaspoons of lemon juice.

1. Light the work candle and start chopping and cutting the fruit for the spell. Many people say that you should also imagine that you are making a romantic dinner for a new love interest.

2. Combine all the fruit into a bowl and stir in the chopped mint leaves.

3. In a separate small bowl, thoroughly mix together the honey and lemon juice.

4. Pour the honey mix into the bowl with the fruit and stir well. You want to make sure that the fruit is thoroughly coated with the honey and lemon juice.

5. As you light the two pink candles, you will want to say the following words:

"This sweet food, prepared with love will bring forth the essence of new love to my life. So let it be."

6. Sit down and enjoy your wonderful strawberry salad.

While you are eating, you want to continue to visualize the new love of your life. You want to think about what you two will do together and how you will interact with each other. Think about the positive and fun times you will have.

Once you are full, you will place leftovers in the fridge and extinguish the candles.

The Start of a Child's Day Spell

This is a spell which you can teach your children. Of course, you will want to make sure they are old enough to perform the spell and understand it. It will also help for you to guide them through the spell, especially for the first couple of weeks or so. To explain the spell to your children, you can tell them that it's a spell which can help make their day more magical.

The best time to start teaching your children this spell is during the summer or on a weekend. This will allow you to be a bit more flexible with your time, which will make it easier when you are rushed to get your children to school.

The ingredients you need for this spell are a pink candle, pink sidewalk chalk, and a sidewalk or area you can use for the chalk. If your children are young, you can use a pink candle with a fake flame.

1. With about two feet between each person doing the spell, stand in a circle.

2. Taking turns, have each child trace their footprints with the pink chalk. If you only have a couple of children, each child can trace their footprints two or three times until a circle is complete.

3. Once the footprints are completed, place the candle in the middle.

4. Have the children pick a starting point within the footprints. However, you want to make sure they are facing East, which is the direction for new beginnings.

5. Once they have a starting point, have the children jump from one footprint to the next.

6. With each time they jump, have your children say or yell these words:

"Great day, good fun! My magic powers will light the way!"

7. After they say the phrase, they should also state one thing they want to do well that day.

8. Once all your children have gone around in the circle, have them stand in the footprints they drew and face the candle.

9. Light the candle and then as everyone is holding hands, repeat the spell phrase at least three times.

10. If the candle needs to be extinguished, allow the children to blow out the candle.

11. Before you put your children to bed, take time to ask them what their favorite moments were during the day. Note what they say and see if you can make a connection between their favorite moments and what they said during the spell.

Strengthening Your Friendship Spell

First, you need to be careful of how you perform this spell. You will need to visualize strengthening your relationship with your friend. However, this can easily turn into trying to manipulate their behavior, which is something you never want to do during a spell. Therefore, it is important to remember to focus on the desired outcome instead of trying to change a person's behavior. For example, if you and your best friend are arguing, you might want to visualize coming to an agreement and moving on from the situation.

For your ingredients, you will need two pink tea lights, a small amount of white and red paint, a paintbrush, a work candle, and five inches of pink cardstock or poster board.

1. Light your work candle.

2. Place the other ingredients around your altar or space.

3. Place the tea lights on the top corners of your poster board or cardstock.

4. Light the candle which you placed on the left of the poster board. As you light the candle, state the following:

"Let the love and light of friendship show through this work. So let it be."

5. Take the white paint and create a symbol of friendship on the paper.

6. Without rinsing your paintbrush, dip it in the red paint and then swirl the red into the painted white symbol. You want to create the color of pink with the paints.

7. As you are creating the color pink, you want to visualize reuniting with your friend. Imagine that two of you having the best times together, laughing, going to the movies, going out to eat, or whatever you do to have fun.

8. Once your symbol is completely pink, you will light the candle to the right of the poster board. As you do this, you will want to say the following words:

"The love and light of friendship strengthen and seal our bond. So let it be."

9. Once the paint is dry, you can extinguish the candles.

10. Place your painting somewhere around your home or leave it on your altar.

Silver

Silver is full of the enigmatic and feminine energy which is closely associated with the moon. This is because many people believe that the moon gives off a silver light. Furthermore, the color silver is known to be really powerful and associated with divine and psychic abilities. Because of this, people often use silver in order to strengthen their psychic abilities, intuition, clairvoyance, and telepathy.

People also use silver to help create a calmness when they are frustrated. This is because silver helps people "go with the flow" a little easier. You can also use silver to help bring luck to various parts of your life and events, such as gambling and finding lost items. Silver is closely associated with the Element of Water.

Lost Is Found Spell

We have all lost something, even if it was temporarily. However, it always seems to happen when we are in a hurry. For example, the moment you are not able to find your keys is when you need to hurry to pick up your children from school or get to the bank before it closes. The Lost Is Found Spell is known to help people find items that they have lost. It doesn't matter if you are looking for an earring which fell off your ear somewhere around the house or your keys, you will be able to find the items with this spell. Of course, you have to also believe that you will locate the items in order for the spell to work.

The ingredients for this spell are a four to six-inch square of silver cloth and two silver candles. You can also use black cloth if you are unable to locate silver.

1. Place one candle on either side of your cloth.

2. Light the candle on the left of the cloth. As you do this, state what you are trying to find out loud.

3. Take 30 seconds to stare intently at the cloth.

4. Close your eyes and visualize the item showing up on the cloth. Imagine that it literally appears out of nowhere. Imagine the item with as much detail as you can remember. Spend the amount of time you need focusing on this vision.

5. Open your eyes and light the candle to the right of the cloth. As you do this, state these or similar words:

"Lost is now found. Lost is now found. What I lost, is now on its way back to me. It is done."

6. Fold the cloth and leave it on your altar. You should place it in a space where you can't easily see it, such as under your candle or tucked away in a corner.

7. Extinguish the candles. You can use them again for this same spell when looking for other items.

8. Give the universe or divine your trust that the item will come to you in time.

Lucky Coin Spell for Gambling

Most of us enjoy a trip to the casino every now and then. There is nothing wrong with this. It sometimes gives us a way to relax and forget about our troubles. However, more trouble can arise when you find you are losing more money than you should while gambling. In order to help increase your luck at winning, you can cast this spell before you head out to gamble.

The ingredients for this spell include one silver candle, a silver coin, and cinnamon essential oil, which is optional.

1. Begin the spell by clearing your mind.

2. Anoint the coin and the candle with the oil, if you choose to use it.

3. Set the coin directly in front of the candle.

4. Light the candle and visualize yourself being successful with gambling. You want to focus on the feeling of winning.

5. Make sure that the heads side of the coin is up and pour a drop or two of wax on top of the coin.

6. Sit the candle back down, grab the coin, and hold it above the flame. As you do this, state the following or similar words:

"Lucky coin and lucky silver, work together to bring me luck and gain. Lucky life and lucky money, I will leave with more than what I came with."

7. Place the coin back in front of the candle.

8. Allow the candle to burn out on its own.

9. Remember to take the coin with you the next time you go on a gambling adventure.

Silver Goddess Reconnection Spell

If you are like anyone else, you might feel that you have drifted from your spiritual path a time or two. When this happens, you can use the Silver Goddess Reconnection Spell to bring you back onto your path. It is important to note that you don't actually have to connect with a goddess or god other than yourself. In fact, the best way to help you get realigned on your spiritual path is to make sure you are reconnecting with your inner self.

While you can perform this spell any time, many people believe you get your best results when you complete it during a new or full moon.

For the ingredients, you will need a white work candle, three silver spell candles, a piece of silver jewelry, and your favorite anointing oil. When you find a piece of jewelry, you can use your favorite piece and it doesn't have to be silver. You can also decide to blend a couple or few anointing oils together to create your favorite mixture.

1. Arrange the three silver candles into a triangle on your altar and light the work candle. Make sure the base of the triangle is facing you.

2. Take the oil and anoint the jewelry. You will then place the jewelry in the center of the triangle.

3. Light the candle, starting with the left base. You will also state the following or similar words:

"Goddess, I greet you at this new beginning point within my path."

4. Light the candle at the tip of the triangle and state the following or similar words:

"Mother Earth, I greet you every day that I walk on top of you."

5. Light the candle at the right base and state the following or similar words:

"Divine feminine, I greet you with every day I breathe along my journey."

6. You will then want to close out this spell by saying the following or similar words:

"I take this time to thank you, goddess, Mother Earth, and divine feminine for this place and time, for reconnecting with me, and your forever presence. Blessed be."

7. Allow the candles to burn out themselves.

8. Make sure you wear the jewelry through your day. You can even choose to wear it for the rest of your life.

Blue

Blue is another color which can help us "go with the flow." It is often thought of as the color of the sky and makes us feel calm, giving us peace and patience. People who struggle with sleep problems will often use the color blue in spells. It is known to be a healing color and helps us resolve tough emotions and allows us to feel stable.

Because the color blue is associated with the throat chakra, we use blue in spells that help us communicate better. It doesn't matter if you are struggling to communicate with someone at work, preparing for a presentation, or trying to communicate with your significant other.

The color blue is also used to help protect us against negative emotions and promote good fortune, confidence, and wisdom. You can also use blue to strengthen your relationships when it comes to trust, faith, reliability, and loyalty. Blue is also used when it comes to meditation, psychic ability, and building our spiritual path. Blue is connected to the Element of Water.

Domestic Conflicts Harmony Spell

The Domestic Conflicts Harmony Spell helps promote home protection. It is a great spell to use when you are trying to bring more positivity and calm into your home. This spell can also be used in order to harmonize your relationships within your home, whether this is with your significant other or roommates.

The ingredients for this spell include two pieces of blue yarn which you can wrap around the candle and one blue pillar candle. You can also use white yarn instead of blue.

For this spell, you will need to have the person whom you are having a conflict with participate.

1. Sit down with the person and face each other. Place the candle between you two.

2. Take a moment to visualize the white light surrounding both of you. This is a way to center yourself for the spell. It is best if you ask the person across from you to do the same thing. If they need help, take time to coach them on how to visualize white light.

3. As you light the candle, start an open discussion about how you both are going to restore harmony within your home. Make sure you use "I feel" statements and are respectful but honest. For example, you might state "I feel that when you bring your friends over I am left out."

4. Throughout the spell, you want to make sure that neither one of you point fingers or blame the other person for anything. Instead, you need to have an attitude of wanting to work through your problems to create better harmony within your home.

5. Once the discussion is over, you both have stated everything you needed to feel heard, and believe harmony has been restored in your home, you may each tie a string to the candle.

6. After you have tied the string, you can extinguish the candle at any time.

7. Make sure you relight the candle every evening where you feel you both had a successful day. You will want to do this until the candle is finished.

Spell to Increase Your Patience

We all struggle with patience from time to time. Sometimes it is because of a bad day, while other times we are overstressed. There are also people who struggle with having patience in general. If you feel that you should increase patience within your life, you will want to use this spell. This spell allows you to assess your stress level within a situation. This spell will also help you create a talisman so you can move through other stressful situations with more grace.

The ingredients you will need for the spell are a blue spell candle, writing paper, a blue mineral stone or opal, and lavender or palmarosa essential oil, which is optional.

1. You will want to do what you can to relax. This means you might want to take a couple of minutes to meditate or breathe deeply. You want to focus on releasing your stress and look at yourself in a more internal manner.

2. If you decide to use essential oil, anoint the candle and then light it.

3. Free write about your stresses which led you to perform this spell. This could be about your relationship, career, friends, politics, or a combination of situations.

4. Take about a half hour to write about what is bothering you. If you start to feel stressed about the situation, look beyond the basics of the situation and into what could be causing these issues. For example, is there something from your past which makes you worried about the situation? Do you fear the situation?

5. Once you feel calmer about your stress, place the blue stone between your palms. Visualize a blue light coming from the stone and going into your body. It starts at your hands, goes through your arms, up to your shoulders, into your chest, etc. Imagine this blue light going throughout your whole body.

6. When you have a clear visual, say the following or similar words:

"Peace and patience flow easily. I will now let go of these old triggers. So let it be."

7. Place the blue stone in front of the candle.

8. Allow the candle to burn out on its own.

9. Make sure to carry the blue stone with you whenever you will need it to help ease your stress, give you patience, and help keep you calm.

"Love Notes to Self" Medicine Spell

In life, it is important that we find a balance between the support and love we give ourselves and what we receive from other people. Too often, people tend to suffer from low self-esteem or lack of confidence, which creates an imbalance between loving ourselves and the love we receive from others. When this happens, we become too dependent on other people.

The "Love Notes to Self" Medicine Spell will help you give the love you need to your higher self. This spell will help create the balance that people desire. One of the biggest reasons we struggle to give ourselves the care and love we need is because we are unable to reach our higher self, or higher frequencies in order to do this. This spell will help us reach these higher frequencies. It reaches into our positive, loving, and peaceful frequencies that will help us work through stressful situations. Therefore, many people believe you should perform this spell days to a couple of weeks before you are going to head into a stressful situation.

The ingredients needed for this spell are a blue candle, a blue pen or marker, small pieces of paper, a small bowl, and a wax seal.

1. You might want to start with meditating, as you will need to relax and quiet your mind for this spell.

2. Focus on your feelings of well-being.

3. Light the blue candle and start writing yourself positive notes of self-love. You should have no less than seven notes, however, you can write as many notes as you want. For example, you might write "I love who I am" or "I am an amazing person."

4. Make sure to fold each message to yourself in thirds so you can completely hide the message.

5. Pour a drop of wax from the blue candle onto the paper to help create a seal. Then, you will press the wax seal down in order to officially seal the message.

6. Once you have written the last self-love note, you may extinguish the candle.

7. Leave these small notes somewhere special around your home or at your altar.

Every time you feel you need a little self-boost, take a message out and read it. You can continue to use the candle to add notes to your bowl as you see fit.

Orange

Orange is a very positive and powerful color, as it focuses on the power of the mind, boosting energy, and physical concerns. The color orange takes the energies of stamina, ambition, and strength from red and energies of cheerful encouragement, optimism, and confidence from yellow. Orange is compared to both the colors within a sunrise and sunset, which means it brings a balance of well-being and warmth.

The sacral chakra is associated with the color orange. This means that the color governs emotions, change, and creativity. Orange is often used in spells to dispel negative emotions, such as abandonment, depression, and grief. It then turns these negative emotions into more positive emotions as the color promotes happiness, eagerness to have fun, and kindness.

Even though orange is often compared to the color of fire, because of its association with yellow, it is an Element of Air.

Challenging Time Encouragement Spell

We all need a little encouragement from time to time. Whether we are focusing on a challenging task or it has just been a while since you heard encouragement, the Challenging Time Encouragement Spell will help you achieve it. When you use this spell, you will feel that you can accomplish your task as it focuses on your character traits and gives you an optimistic outlook on the situation.

This spell is similar to the "Love Notes to Self" Medicine Spell as it focuses on writing encouraging notes to yourself. Like other spells, you should have at least seven notes, but you can write as many as you want.

The ingredients for this spell include one orange pillar candle, one orange spell candle, little pieces of paper, and Bergamot essential oil, which is optional. While you can use any color of paper, many people like to use orange, as it will bring more of this color's energy into the spell.

1. If you are using essential oil, anoint the spell candle with oil.

2. Light the pillar candle and take a few minutes to clear your mind. You want to focus on getting rid of your negative emotions and bring in more positive emotions.

3. Once your mind is clear and positive, start to write encouraging messages to yourself. You can write messages such as "You got this" or "You are doing great, keep going!" No matter what you write, you need to make sure that you agree with what you are writing.

4. Take all the messages you wrote and arrange them in a circle around the spell candle. As you place each message around the candle, make sure to read it out loud, as this will start to give you a boost of encouragement.

5. Once you feel the encouragement, light the spell candle and say the following or similar words:

"All the positive words I speak bring me more joy and light. So it is."

6. Let the spell candle burn out on its own if you can. Otherwise, you will want to light the spell candle again to allow it to burn out on its own. The pillar candle you can extinguish when the spell is done and light it whenever you need an extra boost of encouragement.

7. Take the notes and place them around your home, vehicle, in your purse, or wherever you will see them randomly throughout the day.

Empowerment Bath Spell

While most bath spells are used for purifying and healing, this spell focuses more on giving you courage in order to continue on with a difficult situation.

The ingredients for this spell include one orange candle, one to two tablespoons of orange peels which are dried, five to seven drops of orange essential oil, and any other candles you wish to use for the atmosphere.

1. Take time to clear your mind.

2. Start to run the bathwater. You will want to make it warm, but not too hot. Don't jump in until all the ingredients are in the bathwater.

3. Once the tub is full of water, add the dried orange peels and the essential oil.

4. Light the orange candle along with any other candles you have chosen to use. Shut off all the other lights.

5. Step into the tub and sit down. Once you are in a relaxed setting, take a few deep and slow breaths. Focus on your breathing as you allow the smell to enter your body.

6. Visualize the situation you are asking the higher powers to give you more courage for. Take yourself into that situation and imagine that it all worked out

well. You had the courage to handle the situation and you were successful.

7. Once you have a strong feeling of success over the situation, take a deep breath. As you inhale, visualize an orange glow around your body. When you exhale, imagine that your vision and everything else which was bothering you is leaving your body.

8. Continue to take time and relax in your bath. Enjoy the aroma and the quietness. Once you are done, you can extinguish all the candles.

Navigating Through Sudden Change Spell

Most people struggle with change, whether it is positive or negative. However, people tend to struggle with sudden change more than any other type of change. This is because the change is unexpected, which means you weren't allowed to prepare, which leads you to become unbalanced.

The best way to handle change is to look at the change positively. Unfortunately, this is not always easy to do. Therefore, many people will turn to this spell to help them handle the sudden change. The Navigating Through Sudden Change Spell will help you find your balance and allow you to get through the change by looking at it as a positive direction for your life.

The ingredients you will need for this spell are one orange pillar candle, writing paper, Bergamot or orange essential oil, and an oil diffuser or burner.

1. Pour some of your essential oil into the diffuser and spend a few minutes clearing your mind.

2. Once you feel more centered, take the paper and begin to free write about the changing situation. Start with identifying the change and then move on to why you liked how everything was before.

3. Start thinking about the positive outcomes of this situation. How will this change affect your life positively? You don't need to think about how these outcomes will come about, you just need to open your mind and imagine the positive outcomes.

4. You will want to spend about 15 to 20 minutes of free writing. As you do this, imagine a light of orange shining around you.

5. Once you have finished free writing, fold up the paper and place it next to the candle. Say the following or similar words:

"The wind brings change, which turns into a breath of life. I am now centered and grounded. I am ready for the new blessings. So let it be."

6. You may extinguish the candle and then move it wherever you want around your home. Light this candle every time you feel you need some more encouragement when you are facing change.

Chapter 7: Crystals and Spells

Cultures throughout the world have used crystals and stones in magic for centuries. In fact, they are part of some of the world's oldest spells known to date. The most common spells that were used in the ancient world were spells of protection, good luck, and prosperity. Today, people continue to use crystals in spells because they believe these objects are alive in their own way. As long as we are open to listening to them, they will communicate with us to help better our lives and the lives of other people.

The two main purposes for crystals in spells are for energy and healing emotionally. The spells discussed in this chapter will be organized by stone, just as the previous chapter organized the spells by color. You can purchase crystals in certain shops which have magical objects or online. While it doesn't matter how you purchase the crystals, you want to make sure that you completely cleanse the crystals. You want to cleanse them of their past energies as you want their complete focus to be on your energies. There are several methods that you can use to cleanse your crystals. One way is to run water over them for a period of several minutes. Another way is to bury them in the earth or in salt overnight.

After you cleanse your crystals, you want to recharge them. You can do this by placing them in sunlight. However, you want to make sure that the crystals won't fade if you do this. Another way to charge your crystals is through the moonlight. In fact, many people will charge them during a full or new moon.

You also need to remember that cleansing and charging needs to be done regularly. Some people will do this monthly by following the new moon schedule. Other people will do this quarterly. Whatever you decide to do, you want to make sure to create your own system and follow through.

All of the spells mentioned in this chapter assume that you have already cleansed and charged your crystals.

Amethyst

Amethyst is a purple crystal. There are many different shades of purple, and the ancient Greeks used this crystal as a way to prevent drunkenness. Amethyst is closely associated with the Element of Air. It is known to bring peace and create emotional, spiritual, and physical balance. Amethyst is also known to help people work through suffering and grief. Many people will use amethyst to help resolve conflicts, as it's known to dispel confrontational attitudes. This crystal can also be used for protection and motivation.

Bath Spell for Patience and Flexibility

People will often use crystals in their bath, as it will spread the energies within the water, which means you are basically soaking in the energy from the crystal. This spell is great for anyone who finds that they are struggling with flexibility and patience. There is nothing wrong when you find yourself struggling. However, most people don't like these negative feelings.

A helpful hint when it comes to this spell is to add lavender essential oil into your bathwater. This will increase the strength of the spell. It will also help you to add essential oils into your bathwater.

The ingredients for this spell are an amethyst crystal, preferably medium to large, lavender essential oil, which is optional, and a purple or white candle.

1. Run the water for the bath and light the candle.

2. When the bathwater is halfway full, pour in a few drops of lavender essential oil.

3. While holding the amethyst in your hands, step into the bathtub and place the crystal under the running water.

4. Take four deep and slow breaths. Whenever you exhale, imagine releasing some of your tension.

5. When the tub is at your desired water level, shut off the water and place the amethyst on the floor

beside the bathtub.

6. Spend at least 15 to 20 minutes in the tub relaxing.

7. Drain the water, but remain in the bathtub. This will allow all the negative energy to leave your body, into the water, and then go down the drain.

8. Extinguish the candle and then cleanse and recharge your amethyst before using it for a different spell.

Break Free of Addiction Spell

It doesn't matter what kind of addition you have, you can use your amethyst in order to help yourself break free of your addiction. This is because amethyst is known to have some of the most highly powerful peaceful energies of any crystal. Furthermore, the aim of this spell is to protect yourself from your old, bad habits and help you create new and better habits.

Before moving on, it is important that I take a moment to say that this spell should not be used if you are struggling with a serious addiction to drugs, an eating disorder, or alcohol. If you or someone you know has a serious problem, they need to get professional help. There are no spells which should take the place of professional and legal help. This spell should be used as a step in your recovery process and not a way to beat a serious addiction you are struggling with.

The ingredients for this spell are a purple or black candle, amethyst, a fireproof dish, and a couple of pieces of paper.

1. Light the candle.

2. Meditate or spend some time creating a calm and quietness in your mind.

3. Once you feel centered, take a piece of paper and write down all the negative effects your addiction has had on you, your friends, your family, and any other piece of your life.

4. Hold the amethyst between the palms of your hands and take three to four deep breaths with your eyes closed.

5. Visualize that you are breaking free from all the negative effects of your addiction you just wrote on a piece of paper. As you do this, imagine that the energies from the crystal are heading into your body. In other words, they are starting to change your negative emotions into positive.

6. Place the amethyst in your left hand.

7. Grab the piece of paper with the negative effects on it and place it into the flame of the candle. Once the paper is in flames, drop it into the fireproof dish.

8. As you watch the smoke rise from the paper, say the following or similar words:

"Together, the power of the divine and my energy fuse. This frees me from the trap. My life is now mine. So let it be."

9. While holding your amethyst, take three or four more deep and slow breaths.

10. Grab the second piece of paper and write a list of all the positive effects of breaking your addiction. While you are doing this, make sure you start to feel eager and excited about this new chapter in your life.

11. Once you have finished writing, fold the paper three times and place it in front of the candle.

12. Allow the candle to burn itself out.

13. Keep the paper with the positive effects on you, in your purse, or place it somewhere safe within your home. This will be a reminder of why you are working toward breaking free of your addiction. Depending on how big the piece of amethyst you use is, you can also carry this with you as a reminder and a way to continuously increase your energies.

Moonstone

Moonstone can come in several colors and is an Element of Water. These crystals are typically used for protection. However, they can also be used for feminine intuition, serenity, and fertility.

Fertility Enhancement Spell

This moonstone fertility spell is a favorite, because the crystal works to protect women. Therefore, this becomes an added bonus when casting the spell to promote fertility. This spell aims to help people who are distressed about the challenges of creating a new life. Many people who struggle with fertility start to feel defeated as each passing month brings more disappointment. The result of this can often be more struggle to get pregnant. This is because you are generally able to conceive easier if you are relaxed, calm, and at peace.

The ingredients for this spell are a needle, thread, a shirt that you wear often, a small square of green fabric, and a small moonstone.

1. Take time to make sure you center yourself. While you do this, you will want to hold the moonstone between your palms and focus on your breathing. Take a few deep and slow breaths.

2. Visualize yourself and your significant other becoming parents. Let this energy flow into the moonstone. Make sure you not only visualize finding out about the pregnancy, but also the birth of your baby.

3. When you are done visualizing, turn your shirt inside out and find a spot to place the moonstone where it won't bother you when you are wearing the shirt.

4. Place the green fabric over the moonstone and stitch the shirt and the fabric together. This will hold the moonstone in place. As you are sewing, think of how the fabric and shirt are creating a womb for the moonstone. Remember, this moonstone represents your intentions to bring new life into the world.

5. Once you have finished sewing, hold the encased moonstone between the palms of your hands and state the following or similar words:

"New baby of mine, I welcome you into this life."

6. Put on the shirt and wear it for the rest of the day. You will also want to leave the moonstone in the pouch and wear the shirt as often as you want.

7. Once you find out you have created a new life, you can remove the fabric and moonstone from the shirt. Then, sew the moonstone within the fabric as a keepsake for your child.

Dreaming Moonstone Spell

Dreams are meant to give us messages from the higher powers and the universe. However, when our lives are chaotic and busy, we often find that our dreams don't make sense. This causes us to miss the important messages that we are meant to receive. When this happens, you need to find a way to clear out your clouded subconscious mind. You can do this in many ways, but one of the main ways is through using a moonstone, as this crystal attaches to the moon's psychic and shifting tides.

The ingredients you will need for this spell are four small moonstones to surround yourself with, writing paper, a writing utensil, and a silver candle. While you cast this spell, you can take the extra step and ask for guidance to come your way the night you perform this spell.

1. Light the silver candle. Take a few minutes to create a calm mind. You can do this through meditation or by taking a few deep and slow breaths.

2. If you have a specific question or concern about your dreams, write this on the top of the paper.

3. Place the moonstones in your hands and hold them there. As you do this, visualize your energy flowing into the moonstones. Quietly request that the stones harness your energy, as this will help you receive the messages in your dreams.

4. Take the moonstones and place each at a corner of your bed. As you place each stone, say the following or similar words:

"Through the light of the moon, my dream will flow and allow me to receive its messages. So mote it be."

5. Extinguish the candle before you fall asleep. Make sure to keep the writing paper and pen by your bed so you can record the dreams when you wake up.

Jade

Jade is one of the crystals which has brought its magic through ancient times into the present day. People used to hold this crystal when they were making decisions, as they believed it would help them make the right decision. Today, people believe that jade helps them relieve stress, which is why so many people carry it with them.

Jade is an Element of Water. It provides calming vibes and protection. The crystal promotes wisdom, peace, and balance during times of stress. When you feel that you are stuck in old emotional patterns, this crystal can provide you a release which allows you to focus on establishing new patterns. It brings clarity into a confused mind and soul. People use jade in spells for gardening, abundance, protection, dreamwork, and new love.

Resolving Feelings of Guilt Spell

Guilt is a powerful emotion in our lives. People feel guilty when they make a mistake, said something they shouldn't have, did something bad long ago, are going through the death of a loved one, or even for something they didn't do. Lingering guilt can take away our happiness. It can make us hold on to our negative emotions, which start to take over our positive emotions. This can start to cloud our judgment and decrease our self-esteem.

Sometimes people hold on to guilt because they struggle to apologize. This might be because they are ashamed, they don't know how, or they are afraid the person won't forgive them. When people need to apologize in order to move beyond their guilt, they can lack courage. This is when this spell becomes helpful. The aim of Resolving Feelings of Guilt Spell is to give you the courage to apologize when you need to, which will help you move on with your life.

The ingredients for this spell are at least one piece of raw jade. You can use more than one if you want. You will also need paper, a writing utensil, a light blue spell candle, and a spade.

1. Light the candle and take time to think about why you are feeling guilty. If you need to, you can write down the reasons on the paper.

2. Once you have completed the first step, place the jade crystal in the palm of your dominant hand.

3. Imagine the situation which caused you this guilt. You can then imagine the energies of this situation flowing into the crystal.

4. Visualize yourself making an apology for whatever wrongdoing you did.

5. Visualize the healing energy of your apology flowing into the palm of your non-dominant hand.

6. Place your non-dominant hand over your dominant hand and hold the crystal between your palms. Visualize how the energies are mixing and flowing into the crystal. If you need to repeat this process with another crystal, do so as often as needed.

7. Once this process is complete, take your crystal and find a spot to bury it in the earth. This will release the energies, which will allow you to move on. Of course, if you have other people you need to apologize to, you can repeat this spell as often as necessary. However, you always want to make sure that your apologies are needed in order for you to move on. You shouldn't apologize for anything that you didn't do.

Restoring Balance Spell

Contrary to popular belief, stress can be beneficial. The main reason why people struggle with stress is because it makes people think of their busy lives, everything they need to do, and what bills need to be paid. However, the benefit of stress is it allows us to see when we are emotionally, mentally, and spiritually out of balance. Therefore, when you are feeling stressed, one of the steps you can take is to perform this spell.

The ingredients you will need to restore balance in your life are the yin-yang symbol, which can be drawn, painted, or an item such as a keychain. You will also need two jade crystals.

1. Set the yin-yang symbol on your working space or alter.

2. Take the pieces of crystal and place one on each side of the symbol.

3. While you are focusing your attention on the symbol, take time to quiet your mind.

4. Take your left hand and pick up the crystal to the right of the symbol. Hold it tightly in the palm of your hand.

5. With your right hand, pick up the crystal to the left of the symbol. Hold it tightly in the palm of your hand. Try to make sure you are holding the crystals with equal strength.

6. Place one palm over the black half of the symbol and the other palm over the white half.

7. Take three deep and slow breaths as you hold your palms over the symbol.

8. Visualize how the energies of the symbol and the crystals are restoring balance within your life. Think about the areas in your life which need more balance and allow the symbol and the crystal to help restore this balance.

9. When you are done visualizing, set the crystals directly on top of the symbol. Leave them as is until

you feel that balance has been restored within your life.

Tiger's Eye

We all need to go through necessary change, and tiger's eye will help us. This crystal is also known to help focus our minds, enhance spiritual visions, and bring about clarity. Tiger's eye is known to give us integrity and courage. It can protect us from psychic attacks and is part of the Elements of Earth and Fire.

Tiger's Eye Courage Spell

This spell is known to bring courage in the toughest situations, such as war. It will give you a protective shield which will help you establish internal courage so you can carry on with the task at hand. It doesn't matter what you need courage for, this spell will help you with anything from meeting your significant other's family for the first time to public speaking.

The ingredients you will need for this spell are a red spell candle, four pieces of tiger's eye, and a small cloth bag.

1. Take time to center yourself. You can do this through meditation or simply by taking a few deep and slow breaths.

2. Visualize the situation you are worried about. Take time to imagine that you have completed the task and you are now relieved. Make sure you can feel this sense of relief. It doesn't matter how the task went, what matters is you feel relief and you are proud of your accomplishment.

3. Once you have this feeling, light the candle. Take one of the crystals and place it directly in front of the candle. As you do this say the following or similar words:

"Because I acknowledged my fears, I honor myself."

4. Take the second tiger's eye and place it behind the candle. You will want to make sure the second crystal directly lines up with the first crystal. As you do this, say the following or similar words:

"I trust my words will be guided by my intuition."

5. Take the third crystal and place it to the right of the candle. As you do this, say the following or similar words:

"I believe I can communicate with integrity."

6. Take the fourth crystal and place it to the left of the candle. You want to make sure the fourth crystal directly lines up with the third crystal. As you do this, say the following or similar words:

"No matter the actions of others, I stand in my sovereignty."

7. Allow the candle to burn out on its own.

8. Place the crystals into the cloth bag and carry them with you as you go forth to this encounter. When you are in the moment where courage is most needed, visualize the crystals creating a protective shield around you.

Long-Term Projects Refocusing Spell

When you are working on long-term projects, you can find yourself losing focus. This might be because you are becoming uninterested in the work, as you might feel you need different projects in order to keep yourself motivated. This also happens because people start focusing too much on the little details instead of the whole picture. Whatever the reason is, this tiger's eye spell will help you refocus on your project so you can put forth your best efforts to continue on.

Tiger's eye crystal works for this spell because it is known as the "all-seeing eye." This means that it can view a certain situation from all directions. It will bring the energies from the project back together to form a whole, which will allow you to see the bigger picture instead of the nitty-gritty details.

For this spell, you will need a sheet of blue or yellow paper. Standard size is perfect. You will also need a medium or large tiger's eye crystal, a writing utensil, and several small pieces of paper.

1. Place the yellow or blue paper on your altar and set the tiger's eye directly in the middle.

2. Take the smaller slips of paper and write a phrase or word that describes a part of the project you are struggling with. These struggles can be large or small. For example, you might be struggling with a section of the project, the deadline, or working with someone.

3. When you are done writing down your problems, place your focus on the tiger's eye.

4. Visualize yourself looking at the project from above. Imagine that you are seeing the whole project come together.

5. Keep this vision in your mind for a few minutes, as this will allow your self-confidence to grow.

6. Once you feel that you can confidently finish the project, pick up all the little slips of paper and fold them into the bigger sheet of paper.

7. Take the tiger's eye crystal and place it on top of the folded paper. Leave this on your altar or a different space within your home until the project is finished.

Rose Quartz

Like many other crystals, rose quartz dates back to ancient times. The Greeks and Romans used to use rose quartz in their jewelry. Ancient Egyptians believed that rose quartz would help preserve beauty. Today, rose quartz is known to help bring out compassion and love, as it holds a beautiful pink hue. Rose quartz is often called the love stone and is part of the heart chakra. This stone will help you with any guilt, emotional trauma, resentments, and anger.

Rose quartz is associated with the Elements of Water and Earth. Using this crystal will help you increase your self-esteem and remind you to treat yourself with kindness and forgiveness. The crystal works to teach us unconditional love and enhance our internal awareness. Another reason to use this crystal is to protect yourself from other people's anger and nightmares. It helps restore peace in an environment where there is a lot of conflict.

Self-Confidence and Self-Love Shining Light Spell

We live in a world where people focus on materialistic items. This can often make us lose sight of taking care of ourselves and making sure we give ourselves the self-love we desire as humans. Most people tend to look towards their skills and accomplishments when they need to give themselves self-confidence. While you want to be proud of your skills and what you accomplish, this isn't what it takes to give yourself self-love.

The only way to give yourself the self-love you desire is from within. It occurs when we find peace within ourselves. When we realize mistakes will be made and this is part of life, as it helps us grow into better people. We find our true self-love when we are able to realize that we are worthy of love, no matter what we do in this world.

If you are struggling with self-confidence, self-love, or accepting yourself in any way, this is a spell you will want to perform. Its aim is to help you realize you are worthy of the love you receive from everyone, including yourself. Many people like to perform this spell with small rose quartz, such as a charm or necklace. This allows them to wear the crystal wherever they go, which aids in building their self-love, confidence, and acceptance.

The ingredients for this spell are one orange candle, one pink candle, and one rose quartz crystal.

1. Place the two candles on your altar with enough space so you can put the rose quartz in between them.

2. Take time to meditate or clear your mind with a few deep and slow breaths.

3. After you have calmed your mind, light the pink candle and say the following or similar words:

"The love for myself shines with this light."

4. Light the orange candle and say the following or similar words:

"My self-expression shines with this light."

5. Take the rose quartz and place it between the palm of your hands. As you are holding the crystal, feel the energy from it and visualize the energy flowing from you into the crystal. While you are doing this, you will want to focus on the flames from the candles.

6. Take a moment to remain in the quietness of your mind. Then, take a few deep and slow breaths. Close your eyes and say the following or similar words:

"I love myself. I accept myself. I trust myself. With this light, I shine bright. I let all the world see this new light of mine."

7. Extinguish the candles. Take the rose quartz and wear it or carry it with you wherever you go. Once you start to feel your self-love, self-compassion, and self-confidence growing inside of you, cleanse the crystal for its next spell.

Releasing Unexpressed Emotions and Pain Spell

Have you ever found yourself struggling to find the right words to explain how you are feeling? If this has happened to you, you're not alone. In fact, most people find themselves in this situation during difficult times. While people feel that they are able to get over the unexpressed emotions, they often dwell inside of us. This can create unexpected emotional pain, and we don't know where it came from. Sometimes, we are unaware of this pain, as it is hidden in our subconscious mind. This spell is to help you release these negative unexpressed emotions and pain.

While none of us want to bring ourselves through pain, trauma, and grief, we need to overcome these emotions in order to truly move on and be happy. After all, if we continue to hold on to negativity, we won't have room to increase the positivity in our lives. We need to release old wounds in order for them to heal.

The ingredients for this spell are one pink spell candle, one rose quartz crystal, and lavender essential oil, which is optional.

1. Take a few minutes to meditate or calm your mind after you light the pink candle.

2. Because you want the energy to come directly from your heart, you will place the rose quartz in your left hand. However, you can also take the rose quartz and place it directly over your heart. This is known to help increase the power within the spell.

3. Take three to four minutes and focus on the energies and thoughts that you want to release. You want to focus on the negativity that you have been holding inside of you. This can be done by thinking

about the event, the words you said, or anything that comes to your mind. No matter what the thought is, you need to accept and feel it. You are asking all these negative emotions to come from your subconscious into your conscious mind. This means you are generally unaware of these thoughts. Therefore, they may come as a shock to you, but this doesn't mean they are wrong.

4. Grant your rose quartz permission to heal your negative emotions and thoughts. You can visualize granting the crystal permission and the crystal lighting up with its radiant pink light. You can imagine this light filling your body, starting with your hand, going up your shoulders, and into your chest.

5. Focus on your breathing. As you inhale, bring the energies from the rose quartz into your body. As you exhale, visualize all the negativity being released from inside of you.

6. If you are using lavender oil, anoint the crystal.

7. Find a place in nature to quietly bury your crystal in order for the negativity being held inside of it to release. You will want to leave it there for about 24 hours, as the crystal will cleanse itself.

Bloodstone

While most people think bloodstone is red, it is mainly dark green with spots of red and brown. Since the ancient world, bloodstone crystal has been used to help heal and purify people and the environment around them. Bloodstone is an Element of Fire and brings protection, dismisses negative energy, increases mental clarity, and brings emotional healing.

Anti-Bully Protection Spell

We all deal with bullies. Sometimes we end up being the bully. Whatever the case is, bloodstone crystal can help you overcome the negativity associated with bullying. The way this works is by giving you a circle of protection that will ward off the bully. This is because they will feel like they can no longer affect you. It's always important to remember that bullies thrive on reactions from the other person.

The ingredients for this spell include one black spell candle and one small bloodstone, such as a necklace or charm.

1. Light the black spell candle.

2. Sit down and place the crystal in your lap.

3. You want to start by visualizing the circle of protection growing. It will start as a green orb in your lap. It will then start growing as it encases you inside of it.

4. As the green circle is all around you, imagine there are red flashes of light along the outer edge of the circle. These red lights are a warning to the bully, which will tell them that you are not to be affected by their antics.

5. Continue this visualization until you start to feel a sense of calm and peace take over your body. You can then place the crystal between the palms of your hands and say the following or similar words:

"With Mar's fire and Earth's heart, I receive protection from anyone who wishes to harm me. This crystal will protect me from their stares and words. It will send them on their way. So mote it be."

6. Set the bloodstone in front of the black spell candle and allow the candle to burn out on its own.

7. Bring the bloodstone wherever you will be coming in contact with the person you are trying to protect yourself from.

Strengthening Mother and Child Relationship Spell

Before you think about casting this spell, it is important to remember every relationship is going to have disagreements and rough patches. You should not confuse a regular disagreement with the need to strengthen your relationship. You also need to realize that there are times where you will disagree more with each other than normal. This is typical, and while you can still use this spell as an aid to strengthen your relationship, you also need to realize that this is a part of life.

You also want to be aware that you are not trying to manipulate the other person into behaving a certain way. This spell is used to strengthen the bond between a mother and her child. For example, if you are in a hostile relationship with your mother or child, this is when you will use this spell.

The ingredients in this spell are jewelry with a bloodstone crystal, such as a necklace or ring, and one pink candle.

1. Light the pink candle and place the bloodstone jewelry right in front of you.

2. Take a moment to clear your mind through meditation or by taking a few deep and slow breaths.

3. Take the jewelry and hold it between the palms of your hands.

4. Visualize yourself communicating with the person you want to strengthen the bond with. Imagine that you are able to have a calm and peaceful conversation, even when emotions start to rise. You can be as detailed as you wish in this visual. For

example, you can create a clear conversation within your mind's eye where you both discuss your day or work through the problems you are having with each other.

5. Once you have completed your visualization, turn your focus toward the bloodstone. While holding it in your hands, calmly state the following or similar words:

"Above and below, our relationship will always grow. Above and below, we fill our communication with love and compassion. So mote it be."

6. Extinguish the candle or let it burn out on its own. Take the jewelry and give it as a gift to the person you wish to bond with.

Chapter 8: Herbs and Spells

You can always add herbs to spells. The more you understand herbs and what they mean, the more you will dress your candle up in herbs, as this will help strengthen the power of the spell. While some people like to use a lot of herbs or mix them within a spell, others like to stick to one or two herbs per spell. As a beginner, it is always better to stick with as few ingredients as possible within a spell, as then you can focus more on the energy instead of making sure you are using all the ingredients correctly.

You can find most of the herbs in any grocery within their spices section. However, some of the herbs, such as dandelion and mugwort, might be a little more challenging to find.

Just like you want to charge your candles and crystals, you want to make sure to charge your herbs. There are many methods that you can use to charge your herbs, and sometimes they focus on what herb you are thinking of charging. However, one method that you can use which is easy and can charge nearly every herb is by placing the herb on top of a pentacle, which is already charged. You will then talk about the spell you will be doing by speaking words of intention. You can always call a higher power to help guide you.

You will also want to think about portions when

performing spells with herbs. While some spells don't give you the proportions, it is generally a teaspoon to a few or a tablespoon to a few. You never need to worry about measuring the exact amount when you are performing a spell. In fact, many people say it is best to go with your instincts. When you feel like you have enough herbs for the spell, then you follow this. If you don't feel like you have enough herbs, then you want to add some until you feel that all is well.

Of course, like any other spell, the most important factor is your mindset. You can have well charged herbs and any other ingredients, but if your mindset is not clear and focused on your intention, then your spell might not work or won't work as well. For example, if you have the mindset that this spell might not work, it is pretty much guaranteed it won't work. You have to keep the mindset that the spell you are casting is going to work. You need to have self-confidence and believe in your powers and the powers which are given to you by the universe. You also want to make sure that you always thank the powers that help you after completing a spell.

Nutmeg

Nutmeg is commonly used to help people heal, whether it is physically or emotionally. Again, you need to remember that none of these spells are to be used in place of a medical professional. This herb has also been used to encourage appetite and aid your digestive process. With this said, it is important to make sure that you do not ingest a large amount of nutmeg. It can cause you to hallucinate and is known to be dangerous for pregnant women.

While nutmeg is sometimes associated with the Element of Fire, it is more commonly part of the Element of Air. The spells that nutmeg focus on are bringing about positive emotions, enhancing perception, and enhancing your luck. Nutmeg is also commonly used to create a sense of warmth because it is often associated with cooking.

Home Security Energy Spell

This spell is commonly used when you feel that your home is chaotic. this might be because you are struggling to find a job, find yourself often in conflict with other members of your family, or you are going through a transition. This spell will turn any negativity in your home into positivity by bringing in warmth and encouragement. It will give you the feeling that everything is going to be alright.

The ingredients you will need for this spell include a small drill, one brown candle, nine whole nutmegs, and thick thread or string.

1. Take a few moments to clear your mind. You will then light the candle and place the string in front of you.

2. Take your drill and make a small hole in each nutmeg.

3. Pull the string through each nutmeg. You will want to make sure there is a knot on one end of the string, so the nutmegs don't slip off the string.

4. As you are pulling the string through each nutmeg, visualize that you have all the essentials you need in life. For example, you have food, water, a home, good health, etc.

5. Tie another knot in the string to make sure the nutmeg will stay connected with the string.

6. Place the nutmeg and string between the palms of your hands and say the following or similar words:

"My home gives me shelter. These walls give my home support. Through this, I have all I will ever need."

7. Place the nutmeg right in front of the candle, which you will allow to burn out by itself.

8. After the candle is out, hang the nutmeg somewhere in your home, such as a place where you feel the most tension or fear about change. This could be your bedroom, kitchen, living room, or anywhere else.

An Air Traveler's Good Luck Spell

No matter how often you travel by airplane, you will feel chaos. You will struggle to relax because of all the rules you need to follow, and you will fear what is going to happen if something goes wrong. What will you do if your carry on bag is too big? What will you do if you lose your luggage? There are a lot of worries that go along with traveling. This is when this spell comes in handy. The aim of this spell is to give you the most relaxing flight that you can imagine.

The ingredients for this spell include one whole nutmeg, one yellow spell candle, a yellow piece of cloth, and thin yellow ribbon.

1. Take time to calm your mind after you light the yellow spell candle.

2. Lay out the cloth and place the nutmeg in the center. Then, wrap the cloth around the nutmeg by pulling up all four sides, which you will then tie with the string. You can also cut off any extra fabric.

3. Place the nutmeg between the palms of your hands.

4. Visualize yourself having the most peaceful flight. Let all your worries and anxieties free as you visualize. Imagine that you have all the right sizes of luggage, you go through security without any hassle, and your luggage is never lost. You can even imagine what seat you have on the flight and that there is no

turbulence. You want to create the perfect trip within your mind.

5. Take time to repeat the best trip as many times as you need to. You need to truly feel a sense of calm over you.

6. After you feel calm, you will place the fabric and nutmeg in front of the candle. You will then state the following or similar words:

"With the grace of a bird in the calm wind of flight, my trip will be peaceful and right. So mote it be."

7. Let the candle burn out on its own as you leave the fabric and nutmeg there to soak up the energy.

8. Take the fabric with nutmeg with you whenever you travel. When you start to feel anxious, you can place it in your hand and remember the calming nature this piece releases.

Sage

Sage is known to give you a calm state which can also lead you into meditation. In fact, many people will use sage before they meditate or often sage their home in order to maintain a peaceful nature. Associated with the Element of Air, sage is often used to clear away negative or unwanted energies from our environment or items. It can also give us a sense of healing.

Sage is often used in spells as it can help open up the third eye. It is also known to help protect us, bring us luck, or even help with fertility. Sage is also known to help open up our inner wisdom and helps us handle our grief from loss.

Heal Your Grief Spell

There are many spells which focus on healing your grief after dealing with the loss of a loved one, losing a job, or anything else which causes you grief. Before I go any farther, it is important to state that there is nothing wrong with grief. It is an important part of helping yourself understand and move on from the death of a loved one. This spell doesn't aim to get you over your grief faster. Instead, it helps to turn your grief into something positive by helping yourself and others understand loss, which will help you continue on. It's meant to bring grief into a healthy mindset.

When you cast this spell, you need to make sure that you let all your feelings flow out of you. This is an important step within the spell. Don't allow yourself to push certain feelings to the side or try to cover them up in any way.

The ingredients you need for this spell are a photograph of the loved one you lost, one purple candle, three leaves of sage, an envelope, a writing utensil, paper, and a spade.

1. Light the purple candle.

2. Take a few minutes to focus on the person that you lost. Think about the good times, what your favorite memories are with the person, and their personality. You can think about how they made you laugh and smile. Bring out all the positive memories and emotions that you can about the person.

3. Take time to write a letter to the person you lost. You can say anything you feel that you need to, from the memories you have to how you feel about losing them. You might tell them how you will remember them or tell your children and grandchildren about them. You can write anything you feel you need to in the letter. Don't be afraid to make the letter too long or too short. The focus is on what you want to tell the person.

4. Take the sage leaves and place them into the envelope along with the letter.

5. Seal the envelope with a few drops of candle wax.

6. Place the envelope in front of the candle and allow the candle to burn out on its own.

7. After the candle has finished burning, take the letter to an area in nature where you can bury it with the spade.

8. After you have finished burying the letter, place your hands on the pile of dirt and allow your energy to be placed into the earth.

Sage Tea Longevity Spell

The main aim of this spell is to help you live a healthy and long life. It will also help decrease your stress, as this is one of the biggest magical parts of sage.

The ingredients for this spell include one amethyst, one white candle, one tablespoon of dried sage, writing paper, a writing utensil, and a tea strainer, which is optional.

1. Start to brew the tea and light the candle.

2. Take time to clear your mind.

3. Start to write down the things you want to accomplish in your life. These can be any goals, dreams, or whatever you want to do. In a sense, you will create a "bucket list." For example, you might write down where you want to travel, when you want to retire, if you want to buy a lake home, etc.

4. Once the tea is ready, start to take small and slow sips. Don't drink all of your tea. Choose an item on your list.

5. On a separate piece of paper, write down a description of your chosen item in the present tense. For example, if you took a trip, describe how the trip

went. Where did you travel? How did the flight go? Did you lose your luggage? What sights did you see? Write down all the details that you can think of. You want to act like you actually took this trip and it is fresh in your memory.

6. Once you are finished writing a description, fold the paper three times. Place the paper under the candle holder safely. You want to make sure that the candle flame will not ignite the paper.

7. Take the crystal and dip it into the rest of your tea.

8. Place the crystal in front of your candle where you will allow it to dry.

9. Allow the candle to burn out on its own. Once the candle is out, take the crystal and place it somewhere in your home. You will want to make sure that you can see the crystal often, as this will help you remember the long life you want to live and all the things you want to accomplish.

Cinnamon

Cinnamon is commonly associated with the Element of Fire. Part of the reason for this is because it often reminds people of the Sun, and also because cinnamon is often associated with the warmth of a kitchen as it is commonly used for cooking.

When it comes to spells, cinnamon is often used to help increase your prosperity. People use it in order to increase their luck, financial wealth, and success. Many people use cinnamon in spells that offer protection. This is because cinnamon is known to help banish negative energy which can dwell inside of you or in your home.

New Home Protection and Blessing Spell

Not only do you want to spend time saging your new home prior to bringing in any of your possessions, but you also want to make sure that you protect your things and yourself by blessing your new home once you have moved everything in. Think of this as the conclusion to your moving chapter.

The ingredients for this spell include white vinegar, one white candle, cinnamon essential oil, a funnel, a cloth or sponge, a spray bottle, and a portable candle holder.

1. Add ten to fifteen drops of cinnamon essential oil into one cup of water. Mix thoroughly and then pour into the spray bottle.

2. Fill the rest of the spray bottle up with white vinegar.

3. Place your white candle in the portable candle holder. You will want to make sure this holder is safe enough to move around with.

4. As you light the candle, imagine that your whole home is being filled with a white light of protection.

5. Spray the sponge or cloth with the cinnamon mixture and then go to the door that you use most. Wipe down the door with this cloth. As you do this, you want to imagine that you are creating a barrier so any unwanted energies cannot enter your new home.

6. Walk around your home clockwise from the main door. Wipe down all the windows and doors with the cinnamon mixture. Remember to visualize yourself creating a barrier.

7. Once you have completed this task, head to a comfortable location and sit down. Close your eyes and visualize that all the doors and windows are connecting. This will connect the barriers you created. Together, they will be stronger in keeping out unwanted energies.

8. While you are imagining your walls and doors coming together to create one barrier, you can say the following or similar words:

"Inside of this home is protection which brings peace and joy. So mote it be."

9. Allow the candle to burn out on its own.

A Banishing Blues Spell

We all find ourselves with a case of the blues now and then. This might happen because of certain events in our lives or we feel that the Sun needs to shine for a little bit. Whatever the reason is, this spell can help ease the negativity and bring in more positivity. Again, if you suffer from clinical depression, this is not a spell that you want to use to try to heal yourself. You need to continue to see a therapist and take any prescribed medication. However, this spell can also help you clear your mind and give a little boost of energy, if this is what you need.

Some people like to listen to relaxing music while casting this spell. While this is completely optional, you will want to have one cone or stick of cinnamon incense, incense holder, and one yellow spell candle.

1. Light the incense and the candle.

2. Find a place where you can lay down and clear your mind.

3. Once you find yourself relaxed, say the following or similar words:

"I am raising my vibrations to a higher frequency as I am releasing all my unwanted emotions."

4. Close your eyes and focus your attention on the smell in the room, which should smell of cinnamon.

5. Take a few minutes to visualize a white light surrounding you as you take in this smell.

6. Take deep and slow breaths. As you exhale, visualize your unwanted emotions leaving your body. As you inhale, visualize positivity and calmness entering your body.

7. Continue to visualize this until the candle has burned out on its own or you feel significantly lighter with positive energies.

This is a spell you will want to continue every day until you truly start to feel that the negative energies have left your body and your home.

Dandelion

While many people consider dandelions to be a weed, it is actually an herb which can bring clarity, balance, and help you let go of unwanted emotions and habits. Many people use dandelion in spells which provide wishes. This often comes from the old tale that you are supposed to blow on the dandelion while it is in its white cotton ball phase and make a wish as you see the seeds soar with the breeze. Furthermore, dandelion can help you become confident in your abilities.

Moon and Sun Balance Spell

There are a lot of spells which will help create a balance in your life. This is because it is often an overlooked part of our lives. We often get so busy that we forget to pay attention to our emotional, spiritual, and mental sides, which all need to be well-balanced.

The reason why dandelion is a clear symbol of balance is because of its life stages. It is a symbol of the Sun when it is yellow, and it is a symbol of the moon when it transforms into its cotton ball stage.

The ingredients for this spell include dandelion flower petals, one silver candle, one gold candle, a writing utensil, an envelope, and a piece of paper.

1. Take a moment to clear your mind. You can do this through meditation or by taking a few slow and deep breaths.

2. With the piece of paper on your altar or work space, draw a line down the center of the page. This will create two columns.

3. Label one of the columns "Activities" or "Sun" and the other column "Relaxation" or "Moon."

4. Place the gold candle on the Sun column and light it. Take a moment to reflect on all the activities you have in your life. This can be the things you do at work, with your family, with friends, or by yourself. You can write down your regular errands or anything else that you consider to be activities.

5. Place the silver candle on the moon column and light it. Think of all the ways you care for yourself and relax. For example, this might be reading a book or journaling before you go to bed. You might meditate in the mornings before anyone else is up or you might go for a drive and walk around in nature in order to clear your mind.

6. Look at both of your columns. Notice where you have more information and notice where you need to improve in order to create more of a balance within your life. Think about the adjustments you will need to make and how you can make these changes.

7. Once you have created a plan of action for your changes, fold up the paper and put it in an envelope.

8. As you give thanks to the higher powers who help you with this spell, you can take the dandelion petals and place them in the envelope.

9. Pour a couple of drops of wax from your gold and silver candles in order to seal your envelope.

Wait a few weeks to a couple of months before you open the envelope and take a look at what you wrote on the sheet. As you are reading, think about the adjustments you have made within your life. Notice any improvements with how you feel. You can also take this time to think of other ways to help you continue to find balance within your life.

Spell for Psychic Clarity

Before you perform any spell, you need to clear your mind. We can often struggle with this because the busy lives we live create a lot of noise within our minds. We then start to feel confused, stressed, and our judgments and thoughts become cloudy. The fact is, you don't think rationally when you have a clouded mind. Therefore, it is important to take time and cast spells which will help you clear out the clouded thoughts. This is the aim of this spell.

The ingredients for this spell include one to two teaspoons of dandelion leaves which are dried, one candle which can be purple, blue, or silver, a mug, writing paper, a writing utensil, and a tea strainer, which is optional.

1. Clear your mind. This might be a bit more challenging to do, as you are performing this spell for a reason. However, if you focus on letting go of all the answers you want immediately and let go of your stress, you will be able to clear your mind a bit easier.

2. Prepare your tea and light the candle.

3. As your tea is preparing, continue to focus on clearing your mind and finding a relaxed state. Take a few deep and slow breaths as you do this.

4. Once your tea is ready, say the following or similar words before you take your first sip:

"I open myself for any possibility. I put my trust within my guides that they will lead me, for the good of all and in perfect timing."

5. Start to reflect on your situation. It will help to talk to the higher power, whether this is the universe, God, or a goddess.

6. Take your paper and start to write down anything that comes to mind. This might be what is bothering you within the moment or ideas on how to fix a certain situation. It doesn't matter what comes to your mind. Your higher power is helping you, which means that you might not even realize something was bothering you or even have thought about the idea before. This doesn't make is wrong, it just means that it was in your subconscious and you weren't aware of your guides helping you.

7. Continue to write as you finish your tea. If you find that you finish your tea and you have written nothing down, simply extinguish the candle and come back to the spell in a couple of days.

8. You can place what you wrote down in an envelope if you would like or simply leave it at your altar in case you want to go back to it.

9. If you have written down anything, especially solutions, let the candle burn out on its own. You can always choose to light the candle during the night for a period of time until it is spent.

Thyme

Thyme is associated with the Element of Water. It focuses on feminine energies, luck, and can aid in cleansing your ritual area. To do this, you simply burn the thyme in your workspace. You can also burn thyme in order to cast healing spells, increase your courage, or psychic powers.

Pentagram Self-Confidence Spell

While you might often feel like you are self-confident, you will always have your doubts here and there. It is important that you never doubt yourself while you are casting a spell, as this can create doubt within the spell, which means it won't work as it should. Therefore, when you start to feel self-doubt, you will want to use a spell which can increase your self-confidence.

The ingredients you need for this spell include five thyme sprigs, an image of a pentagram, and a candle. You can use any color of candle that suits confidence, self-love, and self-worth.

1. Take a few minutes to calm your mind as you light the candle.

2. You will start creating the five-pointed star with the five thyme springs. With the first sprig, you will

state something that you are good at. For example, "I am good at painting." You will then place the sprig in front of the candle. You just want to make sure that you have enough space to create the whole pentagram.

3. Before you place the second sprig, think of a time that you showed someone compassion. Say "I showed compassion to _____" and then place the sprig with the first sprig.

4. As you place the third sprig, think of a time you overcame a challenge. State "I overcame a challenge when _____" and connect the third sprig to the second sprig.

5. As you place the fourth sprig, think of a personality characteristic that you are proud of. Say out loud, "I am proud of my compassion." Then place the sprig down in order to continue to the pentagram.

6. As you place the final sprig, think of something that is challenging you in a current situation. Say out loud, "I know I can overcome _____."

7. Now, stand back and acknowledge the whole star you just created.

8. Take a few deep and slow breaths and allow yourself to feel the confidence which radiates from the star.

9. Leave the star there as you allow the candle to burn out on its own.

10. Once the candle is done, take the thyme and go outside. Crumple up the herb as you spread it around the earth.

Thyme Courage Talisman Spell

This is a great spell to cast when you are in need of a little extra courage. This doesn't mean that you don't have any courage within you. It just means that you are a bit nervous about starting a new career, going on an adventure, or starting a new relationship. This courage spell can work in any type of situation in your life.

The ingredients for this spell include about ten inches of orange ribbon, glue, black construction paper, several sprigs of thyme which is dried, a work candle which signifies courage, and a hole punch.

1. Take a few moments to meditate and clear your mind.

2. If you choose to use a candle, as it is optional, light the candle.

3. By using the bottom of a 3 inch circular cup, trace a circle on the construction paper and cut out the circles.

4. Punch a hole in the center of the circle.

5. Take the glue and carefully attach each thyme sprig to the edge of the circle. You want to make sure that a few leaves hang over the edge of the circle.

6. As you are gluing down each sprig, visualize more courage heading your way through the thyme. Imagine how your feeling of courage is growing stronger and stronger every time you glue.

7. Once the glue is dry, place the talisman in between the palms of your hands and continue to visualize the energy you are receiving from it.

8. Thread the ribbon through the circle and then hang it up where you can see it often.

9. You can allow the candle to burn out on its own or gently extinguish it when you are done with the spell. If you do choose to extinguish it, continue to light the candle when you are in need of a little extra encouragement.

Chapter 9: Essential Oils and Spells

When it comes to spells, many people like to call essential oils magical oils. You can easily find essential oils in a variety of stores. You don't need to make sure they are a certain type, however, you will want to make sure that you have a variety of oils, as each oil will give you something different within a spell.

It is important to realize that you don't need to pour a lot of oil into your spells. Whenever you use essential oils, you only need to pour in a couple of drops or so. Sometimes the spell will tell you how much to put in, while other times it will let you decide. No matter what a spell says, you always want to make sure to follow your intuition. This is the same thing you will do when it comes to using herbs in your spells.

Many people like to use essential oils on the wax of their candles. They will rub the side of their candles with the oil. As stated before, because oil is flammable, you want to make sure you don't get the oil too close to the wick. You should also allow the oil to dry on the candle for a period of time before you light the candle. This is simply a safety measure. If you want to anoint your candle with oil, use it as a preparation tool and do this step a couple of hours before you begin your spell.

It is also important to remember that you can add essential oil to any spell, even if it doesn't call for it. While there are a lot of spells which do, and I will soon discuss a few spells which focus on essential oils, they are best known to strengthen the spell. For example, if you want to strengthen a love spell with a pink candle, you might use an essential oil associated with the color pink to anoint the candle. While the essential oil wasn't called for in the spell, you decided to simply make the spell a bit stronger.

Coins Money Spell

There are a lot of money spells which focus on coins. This is because coins are known to bring prosperity due to their symbolism of wealth. When people cast this spell, they need to remain focused on the feeling that they have already received the money. This means that if you want money to be able to save, you think about how you are saving the money. If you need to pay your bills, this is what you visualize doing with the money.

When it comes to your emotions, you want to tap into the last time you found money. For example, you are putting on a coat that you haven't worn in a few months, reach into the pocket, and feel something like paper. You pull it out and notice that it's two $20 bills. This gives you excitement and happiness, as you completely forgot you placed the money in your pocket the last time you ran to the store. When you are able to feel emotions such as this, you're going to create a stronger spell.

The ingredients you will need for this spell include one green candle, a crystal point, essential oil of your choosing which focuses on luck, and three coins.

1. Take a few minutes to clear your mind through deep and slow breathing or meditation.

2. Take a bit of the essential oil and rub it over your pressure points and third eye.

3. Take your carving tool and inscribe your initials on the side of the candle. You will also want to design a symbol of money, such as the dollar sign.

4. Place the candle between the palm of your hands and visualize your power soaking up into the candle.

5. Anoint the candle with the essential oil.

6. Take the coins and place them in between the palms of your hands. Think back to when you found money randomly in your coat pocket or your wallet. Tap into your emotions as you found the money.

7. Place the coins in the shape of a triangle. Make sure you place them face up. You also want the top of the triangle closest to you.

8. Pour a drop of oil at the center of each coin. As you do this, say the following or similar words:

"Just as love attracts love, this money will bring me more."

9. Light the candle and say "So mote it be."

10. Don't remove the coins until the candle has burned out on its own.

11. You will then place the coins where you will see them daily. For instance, you can have one in your wallet, in your kitchen, and in your living room.

Steamy Love Attraction Spell

Whether you are single and looking for a new relationship or want to strengthen the bond with your significant other, this is a spell you will want to try. For this spell, you can mix your own essential oil blend or use your favorite oil which focuses on bringing love into your relationship. When you perform this spell, you don't want to focus on trying to change the personality characteristics of a person. Instead, you want to focus on how you and this person will strengthen your bond.

The ingredients you will need for this spell include one cup of filtered water, your choice of essential oil which focuses on love, a bowl, a small kettle, a bit of dried lavender, and one red spell candle.

1. Take time to clear your mind.

2. Bring forth memories you have where you felt excited and happy. Think about when you felt you were physically attractive.

3. Anoint your candle and the pressure points on your body, such as your wrists, as you are thinking about these memories.

4. Take the cup of water and hold it between the palms of your hands. Focus your attention on bringing love and compassion into the water.

5. Pour the water into a kettle and bring to a boil on the stove. Do your best not to use a microwave.

6. As the water starts to boil, sprinkle any herbs you decide to use around the base of the candle.

7. Light the candle and say the following or similar words:

"My own fashion is love and passion. Through the power of attraction, I call to me."

8. Right before the water starts to boil, take it off the heat.

9. Pour a couple of drops of essential oil into your bowl.

10. Carefully and slowly pour the water on top of the essential oil.

11. Take a couple of steps back so the smell from the essential oils doesn't get overwhelming. While you step back, visualize your power being carried by the steam and into the universe.

12. Allow the water to cool down before you dump it out.

13. Allow the candle to burn out on its own.

Conclusion

By now, you not only know how to charge the ingredients you can use in spells, but you also have a good amount of spells which you feel comfortable casting. You have learned how you can use herbs and essential oils to help bring strength into a spell. You have learned how you can use any type of candle, herb, crystal, or essential oil you want in the spell, as long as it is connected to your outcome and will strengthen the spell. You know that the majority of herbs you find in the grocery store can be used in various spells which will promote productivity, luck, improve self-worth, confidence, and focus on your relationships.

No matter what spell you are performing, you always want to remember to charge the ingredients you are going to use. After the spell, you want to make sure that you cleanse them in order to prepare them for another spell. Of course, if you are using candles, you can continue to use them in order to strengthen the atmosphere when it comes to the spell you performed.

Most importantly, you should understand that you always need to be safe when you are casting spells. You always need to make sure that you keep an eye on a lit candle and be cautious when using oil and other flammable objects. You also understand that you should never use a spell in place of going to a doctor or taking medication. There are no Wiccan spells which can be used instead of seeking professional help. The spells are to be used in conjunction with any medical advice or attention you need.

The purpose of this book was to give you a variety of spells which would help you develop your skills and gifts. However, there are tons of other spells that you can look into using, whether you are a beginner or have been casting spells for a long time. Blessings to you.

References

Book of Shadows. Retrieved 17 July 2019, from https://wiccanspells.info/free-magic-spells/

Carlson, J. (2011). Ways to Charge your Candles. Retrieved 13 July 2019, from https://jesscarlson.com/ways-to-charge-your-candles/

Chamberlain, L. (2018). *Wicca Spellbook Starter Kit: A Book of Candle, Crystal, and Herbal Spells*. Chamberlain Publications. Kindle Edition.

Chamberlain, L. (2017). *Wicca Essential Oils Magic: A Beginner's Guide to Working with Magical Oils, with Simple Recipes and Spells*. Chamberlain Publications. Kindle Edition.

Chamberlain, L. (2016). *Wicca Book of Spells: A Book of Shadows for Wiccans, Witches, and Other Practitioners of Magic (Wiccan Spell Books 1)*. Chamberlain Publications. Kindle Edition.

Curott, P. (2013). How to Cast a Spell | Wicca. Retrieved 14 July 2019, from https://www.youtube.com/watch?v=zfO-4W9uUCI.

Magical Properties of Colors. Retrieved 13 July 2019, from http://wiccaliving.com/magical-properties-colors/.

Sidana, L. (2017). *Wicca: 3 Manuscripts - Introductory Guide, Book Of Spells, Herbal Magic (Wicca For Beginners)*. Kindle Edition.

Warnings & Cautions For The New Wiccan or Witch. Retrieved 14 July 2019, from https://wicca.com/celtic/wicca/cautions.htm

Wilde, D. (2015). Wicca Spells: A Beginner's Guide to Casting Wiccan Magick Spells to Attract Love, Wealth, Health, Divination, and Protection.

Wynd, B. Candle Color Meanings. Retrieved 13 July 2019, from https://wicca.com/celtic/bri/cndlcolor.htm

www.ingramcontent.com/pod-product-compliance
Lightning Source LLC
Chambersburg PA
CBHW071350080526
44587CB00017B/3043